HIT THE GROUND
RUNNING

A WOMAN'S GUIDE TO SUCCESS
FOR THE FIRST 100 DAYS ON THE JOB

LIZ CORNISH

McGraw·Hill

New York   Chicago   San Francisco   Lisbon   London   Madrid   Mexico City
Milan   New Delhi   San Juan   Seoul   Singapore   Sydney   Toronto

Library of Congress Cataloging-in-Publication Data

Cornish, Liz
    Hit the ground running : a woman's guide to success for the first 100 days on the job / by Liz Cornish.
        p.   cm.
    ISBN 0-07-147246-0 (alk. paper)
    1. Women executives.   2. Management.   3. Success in business.
  I. Title.

    HD6054.3.C678   2006
    658.4'09082—dc22   2006002291

1 2 3 4 5 6 7 8 9 0   FGR/FGR   0 9 8 7 6

ISBN-13: 978-0-07-147246-3
ISBN-10:   0-07-147246-0

Interior design by Rattray Design

McGraw-Hill books are available at special quantity discounts to use as premiums and sales promotions, or for use in corporate training programs. For more information, please write to the Director of Special Sales, Professional Publishing, McGraw-Hill, Two Penn Plaza, New York, NY 10121-2298. Or contact your local bookstore.

This book is printed on acid-free paper.

To Papa, Mimi, Sissy, and K-Man . . . and all the Corn-fusion in between.

CONTENTS

FOREWORD

I GREW UP in Berlin during World War II. When I turned 13, our school sent me to a career-counseling session to help me map out my future. My father went with me to the appointment and listened carefully to the counselor's suggestions. We were told that, with my talents and what was available in the city at the time, I should pursue a career in dress design and apply for admission to a special school. I kept very quiet during the whole interview, mentally making other plans.

On the way home, I told my father that I wanted to become an international merchant. I felt that trade brought countries together, contributing to peace. I also wanted to show that not all Germans were bad, and maybe I could help heal the rift once the war was over.

My father's answer was "Oh dear, as a girl, you can never do that. All you can hope for is to type somebody else's letters." That was not what I had in mind, so I went to dress design school instead and forgot about my dream.

But my dream caught up with me about 25 years later. I was living in the United States and started the business of bringing Birkenstock sandals to this country, where retailers first told me, "Women will never wear those shoes." Those two-strapped, wide sandals that no woman would wear just enjoyed their 30th birthday.

If you've picked up this book, you probably have questions about your own career and, specifically, your next moves. You are probably hoping for, considering, or have accepted a new leadership position. Perhaps you're wondering—like I did—"Uh oh, what have I done? And what do I do now?" These are much richer questions to ask than "What did I miss? What did I not do? How did I hold back?"

Leading a national company whose product has literally become a household name and a lifestyle icon has been very exciting. It's also been discouraging, fun, maddening, stressful, thought-provoking, and enriching beyond words. I wouldn't have missed a minute of it. However, there were times when I could have used a resource like the book you hold in your hands.

If you're taking a new leadership position, read and use *Hit the Ground Running*. It is filled with ideas, tools, and practical advice that until now could only be gained from years of life and work experience. Liz Cornish has observed and asked all the right questions of many, many effective leaders—both men and women—and developed a resource crammed with their good ideas and best advice. There's no longer any reason for an ambitious woman to make plans quietly, and with this book as your guide, chances are someone else will be formatting your letters.

Margot Fraser
Founder of Birkenstock
Footprint Sandals, Inc.

ACKNOWLEDGMENTS

WRITING IS LONELY. For a raging extrovert like me, it went beyond a voluntary prison sentence. It was solitary confinement at Alcatraz. Luckily, my wardens were friends and loved ones. "Get back in there, Liz." "Mom, were you up at 4 A.M. again?" "You can do this, Liz." A timely phone call, a quick yell in the front door, or an invitation to dinner was the boost it often took to face another round at the computer. Thanks to Sissy, K-Man, Beth Elliott, Erline Grace, Mike and Beth DeCoss, Joann Guattery, and Dani Barfield.

Long-term projects need a kickstart. Mine came from Kris "what's a year of your life?" Matteri and the partners of The Results Group, especially Rick Brown. Thanks. And there are those who suffered the shortcomings—especially those who read the early, versions of this book: Beth Elliott, Kris Brower, Karen Walker, Alayne Fardella, Kathi Safford, and Beth DeCoss. Special thanks to professional wordsmiths Chris Mohney and Bob Sehlinger, who read and improved lousy manuscripts not once, but ad nauseam. You guys are awesome.

And then, there were hundreds of talented leaders who shared their experiences so that we can all improve. You are too numerous to name, but I am deeply grateful for your skills, the example you set, and your honesty. Special thanks to Doug Silsbee, Allison Cornish, and Alayne Fardella, who are so busy and yet so generous with their time and information. You kept answering when I would have screened my calls months earlier.

Finally, thanks to fellow consultant and friend Chris Sliz, whose extraordinary interviewing skills provided many of the examples for this book and sense of humor kept it fun.

INTRODUCTION

CONGRATULATIONS. As a woman in a leadership position, you deserve it. The challenges are enormous, and the road map is still a work in progress. Perhaps you've had a mentor and some fantastic opportunities en route, but give yourself credit—your own drive, intelligence, and combination of skills got you here. Let's make sure you stay where you belong.

Whether you are just entering the executive suite, taking over a nonprofit, launching a start-up, or managing a new division, this book demonstrates how to "stick the landing" like a world-class gymnast. *Hit the Ground Running* will guide you through the most critical, exciting, and vulnerable time in your career. If you follow the advice in this book, you won't just stick the landing—you'll have reason to take a bow and enjoy a standing ovation.

WHY 100 DAYS?

In these first months, many professional, organizational, and business issues are consciously and unconsciously resolved. Your career can either blossom or begin a slow downward spiral. Whether you've been promoted or newly hired, you will have an overwhelming amount of data to sift through and time-sensitive decisions to make. You'll feel the push to move quickly against the pull to make thoughtful, informed choices. You'll be scrambling to figure out what to do, while others decide whether you have what it takes. You may feel like a newly hatched butterfly eager to take off before its wings dry.

I'll help you take off the right way. Used well, the first 100 days are an unparalleled opportunity to accelerate your success. Your very presence as a new leader shows that you are ready for potential greatness—and you can achieve positive, long-term effects. Unfortunately, a few tactical errors or misjudgments in these first crucial days can instigate a crisis of confidence (for you and others) from which it's tough to recover. This book will explain ways to maximize your chance of success while minimizing your risk in this critical period. Given the overwhelming demands, how should you allocate that most precious commodity: your time?

Life and work for you as a female leader are complicated enough. This book is going to take some of the guesswork out of the first 100 days by providing guidelines for organizing priorities, expanding your capacities, getting a handle on tasks, and applying proven management and leadership techniques. It can be a thoughtful whisper in the ear, a reassuring pat on the back, and—most importantly—a framework for sustainable success.

WHY WRITE TO WOMEN?

As more and more women effectively contribute to America's bottom line, smart decision makers are welcoming and even encouraging us to move up the ladder. Women thrive as leaders, managers, and entrepreneurs—the organizational payoff is enormous. For example, the 25 Fortune 500 firms with the best record for promoting women to high positions are 18 to 69 percent more profitable than the median Fortune 500 firms in similar industries. Consistently, women have proven more likely than men to use leadership styles that produce better worker performance and effectiveness.

Women have an impressive collective track record, and inspirational role models like Madeleine Albright are becoming more common. However, gender representation at the executive level is changing at glacial speed. It's a slowly emerging road, and women must navigate some unique detours.

An Evolving Leadership Culture

First, our culture and women's role in it has changed dramatically in the past two generations. The lessons we learned as a young girls may be deep-rooted but no longer useful. Moreover, our automatic responses are the products of those early years. For example, were you taught that "nice girls raise their hands until called on?" In many company settings, where speaking out is accepted practice, waiting for permission to give your views is the fast track to obscurity and a dead-end career. It is important to understand the strong forces that have shaped us in order to determine what is still appropriate and useful.

Growing up, day after day, moment after moment, we are bombarded with messages that create expectations of who we are, what we can become, and choices we think we have. We unknowingly pick up thousands of clues—unspoken social rules that dictate what is rewarded and what is ignored or discounted by those around us. There are exceptions, of course, but when we grow up seeing who commands the boardroom, stars in big-budget movies, or runs for political office, we make unconscious decisions about our own potential roles. This is how people often self-select who gets to lead and who has to follow.

Instinctively, we tend to either maintain or re-create our culture. It makes our world more predictable and therefore safe. For example, in the movie *The Shawshank Redemption*, lifelong prison inmate "Red" Redding (Morgan Freeman) gives his opinion of the prison walls to fellow inmate Andy Dufresne (Tim Robbins): "First, you hate 'em. Then, you get used to 'em. Enough time passes, and you come to depend on 'em."

What a double bind. The tendency to re-create our world for security's sake often puts the male leader firmly in charge. A woman in the lead is, from a traditional perspective, still an anomaly—both genders are learning how to adjust. Women are continuously bumping up against the familiar "way it's always been." Men are being asked to make room in roles they've historically (and safely) controlled. Giving up top spots in the hierarchy is the modern equivalent of the Neanderthal handing over his club. Meanwhile, women are moving out of the cave. Though more interesting and exciting, it also demands taking risks, toughening up, and preparing to take some hits. Certainly, there are many success stories, but as a culture, we are still in transition. There are times when it would be easier for us bearers of the XX chromosome to dash back inside and hide under the furs.

Even for those women who dominate their arena with talent and drive, outdated expectations remain. For example, notice our fascination with star female athletes. Consider an article by Sheryl McCarthy published in *The Press Democrat* about tennis pro Maria Sharapova:

> It just goes to show that at a time when women athletes are getting more respect than ever before, they are still better rewarded for looking good than for anything else. Female athletes are caught up in a weird double standard. On one hand, we demand that they be competitive, aggressive, and that they win. But we also demand that they exhibit the traditional feminine qualities, even on the court. As we cheer their powerful serves and backhands, we're also scrutinizing their hair and their wardrobe and to what extent they exude that female come-hither quality.

For now, we need to be very good at what we do while still living with traditional expectations of what we should be. No doubt about it—it's exhausting.

Long Odds

Women who make it to the boardroom beat the odds. We are appearing in the corner suites more often, but despite the fact that 46 percent (and rising) of the workforce is female, we represent a mere 3 to 5 percent of the upper echelon of corporate earners.

Of course, the challenge of moving up to those higher offices is daunting. Research—as well as the evidence of our own experience—tells us that the traditional, male-dominated hierarchy is alive and well. The article "Leaders in a Global Economy: A Study of Executive Women and Men" published by the Families and Work Institute , Catalyst, and the Boston College Center for Work and Family noted that women still face "different organizational barriers to advancement, including fewer role models, exclusion from important networks, limited stretch assignments, gender stereotypes, and the tug of dual-career families."

Uneven Rewards

Once we have arrived, women still face lower compensation. Our foremothers fought hard—legal, social, and professional progress has been made—but the pay scale remains lopsided. For example, in 2003 the Census Bureau reported that white men with bachelor's degrees took home $66,000, compared to $37,800 for their female counterparts. As we climb the corporate ladder, the discrepancy often increases. At the vice president level, we still get only 58 percent of the paycheck enjoyed by male professionals. Sounds like a cartoon scenario, doesn't it? Two for me and one for you, two for me . . .

In 1986, I specialized in executive compensation, often consulting for health care organizations. I vividly remember my shock that the director of nursing—often the highest-ranking woman, managing hundreds of professionals—received less than two-thirds the salary of men in positions with the same level of seniority, even if those men supervised far fewer employees. Ironically, the women were often satisfied with their compensation, since they were the highest-paid females in the organization. Outraged, I pointed the inequity out to my boss, who responded, "The other positions are more important to the hospital." More vital than the nursing staff? Remember that the next time you're in intensive care.

Things have progressed since then, but they haven't done so either quickly or uniformly. One friend, who is rapidly advancing in her male-dominated organization, was recently told that she should be delighted with her compensation. Why? Again, because she is the highest-paid woman in the company. She is paid less than her male counterparts who have far less responsibility. She even makes less than one of the men who reports to her! Two decades have passed, and yet gender still affects level of pay to a startling degree.

Double Standards

Women are often caught between what leadership requires and what is classically expected of the "fair sex." It's relatively safe ground to mentor, empower others, encourage innovation, and promote collaboration. However, if leadership calls for a woman to be direct and authoritative, you have a bitch on your hands! We've been too brainwashed by Sleeping Beauty and sitcom housewives to appreciate a female Jack Welch.

Tough-minded, strong-willed women run counter to our cultural icons of femininity, and the friction can cause discomfort and resentment. A traditional, hierarchical style of leadership can be very risky for us. Men have more latitude and, frankly, more room for error. Society is more forgiving of male managers and allows them a wider range of leadership styles. Men walk a beam—women, a tightrope.

Internal Noise

I rarely interview a woman executive, especially one with children, who does not feel conflicted about her multiple roles. The old expression "Men go about putting their careers together, women go about putting their lives together" is still true for many of us. We have to juggle our roles as leaders, family members, friends, and nurturers, both at work and at home.

Women have more professional and personal options now, so we wonder if we are making the right choices. If we take off to see the school play, we feel guilty. If we don't see the play, we feel guilty. Or we drown in a sea of shoulds: "I should attend this meeting. I should be a better daughter. I should get some exercise. I should quit saying *should*!" If we stay late at work, we worry about our parents, kids, or significant others. But if we make time for these important people, then we're not being productive. The internal dialogue is deafening, and the internal critic is tough to satisfy.

Women also seem to be harder on themselves for longer periods of time than men are. Perhaps that tendency is hardwired into the gender, since it often emerges early in childhood. For example, my son Kenneth and daughter Carolyn are both soccer players. Several years ago, they had simultaneous games on parallel fields. Carolyn berated herself for her lousy game—she had, after all, missed an easy score and turned over the ball a couple of times. Meanwhile, Kenneth, playing goalie, literally swaggered off the field. He said, with excitement and in all seriousness, "Mom, did you see how many goals I almost blocked?" His team had lost 18–0.

Intense Scrutiny Equals Increased Stress

Imagine watching a football game that had 21 refrigerator-sized male players and one woman—perhaps at fullback. You're going to notice to that female player simply because her presence is unusual. It's human nature to pay more attention to the new, unique, or curious. The increased scrutiny can be stressful to the new woman leader.

For example, a few years ago, Anne flew to the Arctic Circle for a 10-day solo canoe trip. She searched maps for the most remote areas, thinking they would be free of humans but rich in wildlife. She didn't realize that a woman traveling alone in a wilderness area would fascinate the locals. Arriving in the town where she had hired a bush pilot to fly her to the starting point, people gathered, and the buzz began.

"You're so small! How are you going to handle the bears?"

Several men also traveling alone were launching out of the same town. Liz mentally did the math. She weighed 120 pounds, and the men were roughly 170 each. Fifty pounds. What possible difference would that make against a 1,200-pound grizzly? The point was not her size; the point was her gender. People noticed and were surprised, then instinctively skeptical—even though the men's extra size would have just meant a bigger meal for the bears.

In leadership, the same is true. Despite the great strides of women in management, our numbers are still small. Sometimes the unspoken assumption is that women don't take leadership roles because they can't perform. Colleagues and staff are watching and wondering, "Can she handle this?" Even if a woman is comfortable with her position of authority, others may not be as pleased with her presence. Women leaders experience more stress than their male counterparts because they must expend more effort simply proving themselves.

More than just leaders, female executives are women leaders. As Clare Booth Luce once said, "Because I am a woman, I must make unusual efforts to succeed. If I fail, no one will say, 'She doesn't have what it takes.' They will say, 'Women don't have what it takes.' " No pressure there! Regardless of how good-natured or confident you are, the psychological and emotional strain of this level of attention will add up.

Less Relaxation

According to an article called "How Consumers Spend Their Free Time," published on forbes.com, men average 39 more minutes of free time per day than women. Think of what you could do with those 39 minutes. Sleeping, reading, hanging out with loved ones . . .

Speaking of loved ones, if you are married with children, you can expect to give up 75 more minutes a day than fathers do, according to the forbes.com article. As the *New York Times* reported in an article called "Survey Confirms It: Women Outjuggle Men," two-thirds of working women prepare meals and do housework on an average day, compared to 34 percent of men helping with meals or cleanup and 19 percent doing housework.

Self-Imposed Limits

Some executive women unintentionally limit themselves with their choice of leadership style, communication habits, response to criticism, and negotiation techniques. They must work hard in order to recognize, analyze, and eliminate these self-defeating behaviors.

So you see, women deserve special attention and advice because they face different challenges in their first 100 days. No matter your particular situation, how you start will determine the long-term success of your leadership tenure. A thoughtful approach and execution during your first several months can produce amazing and lasting results.

ABOUT THIS BOOK

Hit the Ground Running is the result of more than 25 years of direct leadership coaching experience, as well as hundreds of interviews with successful female and male managers—CEOs, presidents, elected officials, executive directors, top military leaders, and others.

Like most busy women in leadership, you are probably eager to get going. This book is packed with checklists, suggestions, and tools for a powerful start. For example, we'll discuss how very talented women unwittingly hamper their own efforts and what to do about it. You'll get ideas for establishing your credibility and finessing a challenge to your authority.

You'll also find suggestions for organizing your learning period and setting the right tone with your staff. We'll take a look at how your early efforts should vary depending on your situation. After all, a business growing like wildfire requires different messages and activities than a company slowly losing market share.

Time Lines

Don't let the 100-day time line make you hyperventilate—it's flexible. Naturally, your circumstances will dictate your real day-to-day (and month-to-month) milestones. Newly promoted (rather than newly hired) women will know their local operational issues, but they may spend more time managing awkward relationships. In either case, you'll need to budget your time wisely. Though you should consider the 100 days a guideline rather than a deadline, it's still prudent to apply these methods and concepts as quickly as possible—whether it takes you three weeks or six months.

How **Hit the Ground Running** *Is Organized*

Each chapter includes the following:

- JumpStarters—key coaching tips for setting up and launching your first 100 days
- Frank discussion and concrete suggestions on how to meet the unique challenges that face the female leader
- Tools to help plan your activities and approaches to help maximize success while minimizing risk
- Chapter checklists to ensure you're done!

Chapter 1 encourages you to take charge of your start before your first day on the job. We'll provide a plan for performing due diligence to find out all you can about your new job and organization. This chapter also provides ways to observe meetings, which are a rich forum for learning critical organizational and cultural information.

Chapter 2 helps you examine your capacity for leadership—hopes, strengths, weaknesses, triggers, your personal "shadows," and other core concepts. It also explains how being authentic—staying true to yourself and what you believe—is one of your most critical strategies as a new leader. Personal authenticity builds trust and credibility, while acting at odds to your core principles creates internal stress and external friction.

Chapter 3 outlines the elements of a successful "going-in strategy," starting with your entry plan. You'll learn why and how to develop leadership anchors—the rules of engagement you need in any management position—as well as a fail-safe support system to maintain strength during critical times. All of these points form the foundation for a woman's guide to negotiation, which will help you get what you need to succeed right now while keeping the door open to further negotiations down the road.

Chapter 4 helps you plan your first day. You'll find plans for turning first impressions to your advantage. New leaders live in a fishbowl, and new women leaders are the most exotic fish of all. This chapter also describes the meetings you need to have, the messages to convey, and how to structure your conversations. Your first interactions are the proverbial writing on the wall. Getting them right avoids the hassle of damage control later on.

Chapter 5 highlights the activities and priorities of your first 50 days. This chapter is a guide for confirming or correcting your first impressions, managing your relationships, and establishing your message. Whether you are freshly hired or promoted from within, this chapter will show you how to take advantage of being new to the job.

Chapter 6 discusses the importance of a transition team—a temporary advisory panel for your first 100 days. You'll learn how to create, select, and get the most out of this extremely valuable resource.

Chapter 7 tackles your second 50 days. It helps you narrow your options, set priorities, and build momentum for your plans. The "honeymoon" will end, and this chapter discusses how to manage the inevitable challenges with individuals and your team as you move forward with your agenda.

Chapter 8 describes special circumstances, such as typical setbacks and how to overcome them. It also explains how you'll know—and what to do—when your transition is complete.

Lastly, the **Appendix** contains two supplementary sections. The first, "Why Organizations Should Care," outlines what companies can do to facilitate a new leader's success and details the effective programs I've seen for leadership development and succession planning. The second, "100-Day Accelerator," provides a host of resources, examples, and fill-in forms linked to the main ideas and exercises in each chapter.

A FINAL NOTE

Of course, no book can replace your own good judgment. So much of a leader's work requires careful assessment of unique situations and complicated strategic issues. As Terry and Lenny Russell wrote in *On the Loose*, "Beauty is not in the book, and adventure is not on the map." Good leadership is not in a book, but you can get some great scouting advice from those executives who have successfully traveled the same road you're starting down now.

In a 2004 leadership conference, David Gergen (a political journalist who also served in the administrations of presidents Nixon, Ford, Reagan, and Clinton) joked about his colleagues' reaction to women executives, saying, "I'm so glad my daughter is a professional go-getter, and even happier my wife isn't." My hope is that by the time my 14-year-old daughter launches her career, female leadership role models will be everywhere—and this book might be just an amusing relic of a bygone era.

CHAPTER

Take Charge of Your Start

IN THE SPIRIT of reality TV, let's start with a scary statistic: 4 out of 10 newly promoted managers fail within 18 months of starting a new job, according to Manchester Consulting. They are removed, perform significantly below expectations, or quit. Four out of 10! That is a huge risk in terms of time, money, and heartache. But if you didn't want to take a risk, you wouldn't have taken the job, right? Now that you have the job, let's make sure you ace it.

We'll begin by setting up for the first 100 days. There are some important steps you can take to "bust out of the gate snorting," to borrow a phrase from my Kentucky horse-racing vernacular. The key to a successful start is to create it yourself, and these first three chapters will show you how—by doing your homework, exploring your capacity for the specific job, and developing a going-in strategy.

JUMPSTARTER: *START WORKING BEFORE DAY ONE*

Don't wait for your official first day to get started. Maximize the time you have beforehand. First, you'll want to finish the *due diligence* (research and analysis of the company) that began during your interviews as you asked questions about the job, the company, and your colleagues. Take an honest look at yourself relative to this job. By doing so, you can develop strategies for a dynamic start, create a fail-safe support system, and develop your *anchors*. Discussed in depth in Chapter 3, anchors are your rules of engagement—the blueprint of conduct you need for yourself and from others to be effective in your position.

INTRODUCING LIN

Lin has been offered a new senior staff position. With a successful track record, the right educational credentials, and 10 years of experience in the public works field, she is well equipped to take the job. She is liked by her staff and colleagues because she listens and follows through. However, she knows the position is loaded with challenges.

First, Lin is transferring from human resources, a very supportive environment, to a highly technical department known for its cavalier style. In fact, the department's top staff recognized the need to shift to more inclusive management, and they actively recruited Lin as part of that strategy. Second, since she is an HR expert rather than a technician, Lin is new to the department's technical work. Last, some awkward relationships will need to be smoothed over, since Lin will be managing people who competed for her job—and the union is wondering about her political savvy. Although her boss is encouraging, his focus is on high-level policy issues, taking him out of the office most of the time. She can expect challenges—both overt and subtle—from some of her peers.

Can Lin do it? Was it the right move to take this job? What does she need to do to set herself up for success and get off to the right start?

In these first two chapters, you will meet three characters—Lin, Allie, and Elaine—whom you will bump into periodically as they move through their own leadership start-ups. Their stories will illustrate the real-world application of the tools described, and they'll demonstrate how a thoughtful approach in the early phases can both maximize success and mitigate big problems later on. Better to learn from their mistakes than make your own, right?

Avoid Red Convertible Syndrome

The recruitment stage is like a night at the Oscars—everyone wants to appear at his or her best. This mutual wooing is important, but you must take advantage of the transition time. If you don't, you will miss your best chances for a strong start. The first step is to avoid a very common condition: *red convertible syndrome.*

In an effort to recruit the best candidates, many companies, departments, and potential bosses paint an overly rosy picture of the job or the organization. Like the allure of a hot-looking ride, this image can sweep you away with glamorous first impressions—when what you should really do is take a thorough look under the proverbial hood.

For example, caught up in the frenzy of the mid-1990s telecom boom, Valerie took a job as the vice president of a wireless loop technology start-up. With the promise of stock and the possibility of an initial public offering, she jumped in with both feet. Certain of an astronomical payoff (and a tropical early retirement), she was shocked when the company failed to close round after round of funding. Ailing finances led to layoffs. The company shut its doors less than two years after she took the job.

Don't fall for the red convertible. Don't be so enticed by the promotion or reputation of your new employer that you fail to ask the tough questions that could expose big issues. Many very talented people have missed the warning signs. They either moved cross-country before discovering the job had a snappy title but no substantial authority or learned too late that their new company was in a financial tailspin.

Fran is one example. Aggressively recruited by her charismatic new boss, she left New York for the West Coast to work at a rapidly growing biotech firm. Within two months of Fran's arrival, the boss quit to join a start-up, leaving her to report to a new CEO. The new boss quickly reorganized and snatched away most of Fran's major responsibilities.

JUMPSTARTER: *DO YOUR HOMEWORK*

Before you begin your new job, dig for data. Use multiple resources to conduct a thorough analysis—you've got to talk to real human beings in addition to reading through records and press clippings. Current staff, former or retired employees, vendors, analysts, and outside consultants are all potentially rich sources of information. Documents such as strategic plans, annual reports, employee surveys, task-force reports, business press, and board minutes will fill in the gaps. Approach your new workplace like James Bond sizing up a mission. You need to know everything there is to know.

My Ph.D. colleague says that good research requires you to "keep reading until you are mildly annoyed by the repetition of information." Does the data you read match what you learn from others and your own assumptions? See Accelerator 1A in the Appendix to consider what you need to learn. At a minimum, learn everything possible about market performance, organizational issues, your new position, and the people and culture.

Remember, there's nothing worse than watching your career go into a slump over a problem you could have dodged with a little homework early on. If you've been promoted and already know the company, there's still plenty to learn about your new boss's style, other departments, and operational issues. For example, Sheniqua had a strong labor-management background. She passionately believed in the value of employee unions and in creating collaborative partnerships. While applying for a management job at a hospital, she discovered the executive team was planning a campaign to encourage employees to decertify the unions. She knew instantly the job would be a poor fit for her.

Learning the background of key people provides useful information that you can use to establish rapport. "Frank, good to meet you. I've already heard about your great work resurrecting the Brown account." The road to success may be packed with surprising obstacles, which a good knowledge base will help you negotiate. Knowing the relationships among people could have avoided the following near-fatal gaffe.

One new leader of a large financial firm began spouting off righteous frustration about a particular executive. A smart insider quickly pulled him aside to explain that the audience for this outburst was a close-knit web of family and friends. The entire company was riddled with in-laws, golfing buddies, and business-school pals. There were all kinds of ways for gossip to get back to exactly the wrong pair of ears.

And, if you are the first female there and expect some resistance, there may be "preemptive moves" you can make to solidify your leadership.

If You're the First Female There

When Karen was promoted as human resources director at the paper and pulp division of a large manufacturing company, she knew she had to build credibility immediately. The organization was predominantly male and had offered few opportunities for woman executives in the past. Before setting foot in her new office, she rode with truck drivers, walked with foresters, and spent time learning jobs on the manufacturing floor. By the time she started working in her office, most of the people in the division knew her. She wasn't "the new HR director"; she was Karen.

Finally, do enough reading that you can ask the right questions and establish credibility quickly.

If You Do Read the Written Word

In discussing the first interview for her job, the CEO of a $7 billion enterprise remembered that after studying the company's strategic plan, she referenced it in a question-and-answer session with the board panel. Imagine her shock when her very prestigious board asked, "What plan?" They were clueless that a strategic planning process had even occurred! That one comment spoke volumes to the prospective CEO about her potential authority. The board was a "rubber stamp"—the staff really led the organization. The time she originally thought would be necessary to sell her ideas could be redirected to operational challenges.

LEARN HOW TO WORK WITH A BOARD OF DIRECTORS

Do you have 16 board members? Then plan on 16 new bosses, and realize that you need to understand how all of them operate. Learning to tame this schizophrenic octopus is often the most challenging part of an executive's professional life. Make it a priority to find out what makes your board tick by setting aside one-on-one time with each of them.

- What has been the historic role of the board in setting organizational direction?
- How seriously does the board take its oversight responsibility? Is the organization led by the board or by the staff?

- What level of business experience do board members have? (This is particularly important in the public and nonprofit sectors.)

Board Relations

- What relationships, political/personal alliances, or cliques exist among the key players?
- Who's an insider, and who's an outsider? (Identify the power players as quickly as possible.)
- What's the relationship between the board and the executive staff?
- How are issues resolved, and how are decisions truly made?

Individual Board Members

- Why are they involved with this particular organization?
- What do they want to contribute?
- What do they expect of you?
- What can they tell you about the organization before you begin?

Finally, what is the female representation on the board? You'll want to know because, first and most obviously, there may be a connection between the number of women on the board and how well the culture supports the advancement of women in the company. Dr. Judy Rosener, in *In Women on Corporate Boards Make Good Business Sense* (womensmedia.com/new/Rosener-corporate-board-women.shtml), also points out that women in the boardroom increase the likelihood that women's market issues will be identified and addressed (cars have a place for your purse) and that governance will improve (the sexist language and sexist jokes disappear, and more substantive questions get asked). Women, as the relative outsiders, tend to ask different questions that can enhance conversation and expand perspectives. Perhaps not surprisingly, women are more likely to consider the "needs of more categories of stakeholders" and examine a "wider range of management and organizational performance." Roy Adler of Pepperdine University, tracked 215 Fortune 500 companies and found that "companies that smash the glass ceiling also enjoy higher profits." Therefore, female board representation can provide important indicators of both your own advancement opportunities and the likelihood of the company's overall success. After all, if you're taking the chance, you might as well be surfing the right wave.

Lastly, make a point of getting to know the board secretary, who probably has a wealth of organizational history to share.

PAY ATTENTION TO YOUR GUT FEELINGS

Once you've assembled all your research and talked to sources high and low, it's entirely possible that you'll still have the feeling you're missing a key detail. Maybe you have a hunch or a nagging doubt, or maybe your perspective gives you insight that organizational insiders lack. Maybe you're just nervous—but then again, maybe you are missing something. During the "total quality management" era, when widespread use of statistical analysis drove decision making, it was typical to see signs posted in offices that read, "In God we trust, everyone else must have data." Instincts and gut reactions are data. Pay attention to them. They don't have to rule your life, but intuition can be as valuable a resource as any other.

JUMPSTARTER: *USE MEETINGS AS A LEARNING TOOL*

American workers often believe that meetings are a terrible waste of time. However, early in your tenure, meetings are a gold mine of information. The time a group spends together will teach you a lot about culture, morale, productivity, and the work itself. Grab the chance to observe meetings before you begin or just after you start. Your presence will affect the dynamics, but you can still learn a lot. If you are being promoted and know the organization well, use the questions provided in this section as a tool for watching with "fresh eyes."

Purpose and Outcome

Learn why meetings take place and how successfully they achieve their objectives. Are the meetings a good use of participants' time?

Seating

Observe the room arrangement and where people—especially the women—sit. Some will move to the back of the room or opposite the leader, while others tend to sit closer to the authority. This can give you an early but enlightening glimpse of the power dynamics.

For example, Kate, a new manager running her first meeting, noticed the distinctive clusters of "ties" (executives), business casual (supervisors), and blue uniforms (line workers). This was an early but accurate indicator of the lack of trust between levels of authority, and she realized she has her work cut out for her.

When observing a regularly scheduled meeting for the first time, ask whether people usually sit in the same place. It's possible that the established seating routines reflect entrenched behaviors. Remember that you are only forming a hypothesis. Don't assume that Frank's position in the corner means he's defiant. Maybe he's left-handed.

Notice, too, your most comfortable position. Does it reflect your desired management style? Many women avoid taking "command" at the head of the table, choosing the more team-based sides or a "round" table. However, the job may require you to take firm charge initially—putting you front and center. It's useful to recognize, then proactively adjust, your natural seating tendencies.

Status

In many organizations, there is a grim satisfaction to receiving meeting invitations—the busyness is a powerful statement about the person's perceived value to the team. As you observe, you may spot these "meeting professionals." They show up a lot, but you have to wonder how much work they really accomplish. This might provide you with insights about accountability and what the organization will tolerate.

Readiness to Engage

Notice the spirit in the room both before and during the meeting or how attendees' behavior changes when the leader enters or leaves the room. If you spot inconsistencies, you will need to dig deeper to get the real story; there are probably trust issues among the group.

Giving and Receiving Information

Carefully study the quality of information exchanged. Do participants appear prepared for the meeting? If staff are supposed to absorb information, do they? Is the information relevant to their jobs? In the meeting, observe how vigorously they question and volunteer information.

Take special note of how women participate in the meetings. Are they forceful? Reserved? Naturally, it won't determine your own actions, but it can be useful to note how other women conduct themselves, especially if they are in the minority.

By the way, notice interruptions in meetings. Several studies have proven that when men speak with men and/or women with women, not only are there relatively few interruptions, but they are usually balanced. However, if it's a cross-gender conversation, there are more overall interruptions, with 96 percent involving men interrupting women.

Problem Solving

Watch how actively everyone engages in solving the articulated problem. See if you can spot patterns of blame, evasiveness, or rigidity. Are discussions honest and productive? Use your intuition to guide you. For example, meetings were held in one health care organization to strategize how to adjust operations in response to the frenetic changes in medicine. Two powerful surgeons consistently and deftly moved the conversation off the agenda. Finally, a savvy observer realized that it was an unconscious but effective way for the doctors to avoid the irritating changes.

Influence

There are always informal power structures. Sometimes they are subcultures, even cliques. Notice who influences the conversations and decisions and to whom people look for direction and information. Recognize the extent to which the group allows the informal leader to exert influence. Informal leaders are often sought out for their expertise, ability to listen, capacity to influence others, and/or personal qualities such as charisma or sense of humor. Such people are often the first to recognize or learn of approaching problems within the organization. They are an extremely valuable commodity and can be your strongest allies— or most persistent critics. Use meetings as one way to figure out who they are, because they are good candidates for your transition team (discussed in Chapter 6).

For example, one city sponsored a controversial ballot measure that included a tax increase. A successful measure would guarantee powerful gains in public safety and youth services. Internal momentum for the measure ground to a halt when an extremely influential employee withdrew his support. The external campaign work stopped until harried management could regain the employee's backing. Observing meetings will help you identify these powerful players.

Nonverbal Dynamics

Take advantage of most women's natural ability to read nonverbal dynamics. What conscious or unconscious "payoff" does the influencer need? Does he or she want attention? To maintain good relationships? Action? When you eventually seek support, you can articulate your ideas so that the influencer is more receptive. For example, if Frank likes action, you might say, "Frank, this initiative is important because it will speed up production and yield faster results." Compare that to how you might approach Hank, the influencer who hates conflict. "Hank, this initiative—which will speed up production—is going to reduce the frustration people have been feeling around here."

Notice the difference between what's said and the nonverbal cues consciously or unconsciously demonstrated by everyone present. As anyone who's ever raised a sulky teenager will tell you, nonverbal clues can often communicate a lot more than what's actually said out loud.

For example, a union executive team extolled a highly collaborative style of decision making. However, when attending their meetings, I noticed that the top person always sat at the head of the table—a habit of 20 years. One day, in a devilish moment, I took her spot. She became visibly uncomfortable. When I excused myself for a break, she moved into my chair. Not surprisingly, a careful observation of the conversation revealed her authoritarian decision-making style. Her power rested in her nonverbal behaviors and what she did not say. She was Attila the Hun in business casual.

Conflict

It's possible that people may be on their best behavior when you first observe meetings. Watch closely to see if there are signs of disagreement in the group and how conflict is resolved. Are disagreements articulated in an issue-focused, respectful manner? If there is spirited debate or argument, do the women readily participate? If conflict isn't resolved at the meeting, notice what, if any, follow-up activities are established to settle outstanding conflicts. If there is no clear conflict, there's a tiny chance you're surrounded by robustly compatible employees. Unfortunately, it's far more likely that the organization supports a culture of silence that represses conflict and disagreement at the expense of efficient problem solving.

Unconscious Behavioral Patterns

Group norms—behavioral patterns—are a fascinating aspect of organizational culture. Sometimes they become so habitual that a group is unaware that they exist until called to members' attention by an outsider. This is especially significant when the differences between men and women are examined. Many norms begin for no apparent reason, and many are based on outdated sexual stereotypes but continue for stability's sake. They are easiest to notice when you are new to the organization or make a conscious effort to observe objectively. Behaviors are entrenched in everyday working relationships, and meetings are an excellent way to discover them.

Some typical examples of group norms to observe in meetings are as follows:

- **The behavior of the highest authority.** For example, the ranking leader may tend to arrive last—maybe even a little late—to meetings as a signal of his or her importance.
- **The use of humor.** Humor (or sarcasm) can be used in a variety of ways. Some are productive, while others make for subtle weapons. Notice the way humor is used in the group. It can be a way to break the ice and have fun or a sly technique for challenging the hierarchy.

As you conduct due diligence and observe meetings, you will begin to form a working hypothesis about your overall entry plan. Those words are carefully chosen, because although you may recognize symptoms, you cannot really understand the underlying conditions until you start the job.

For example, while observing a meeting, you may notice poor communication among the national sales force. It's not until after you start that you learn the competitive pay structure discourages teamwork. "Last year, I tossed Frank three great ideas

WHAT'S IMPORTANT TO WOMEN

Women are often turned off by hierarchy and therefore fail to look for the power cues that meetings can provide, missing the chance to establish key relationships. If hierarchy does not inspire you, try checking with people you trust about important dynamics that meetings can reveal.

While men are fighting for airtime, women are more likely to stay quiet. They risk losing their voice and their power. Once you become an active team member, monitor your level of participation.

for boosting his numbers in a couple of poorly performing stores. He used them all, took the top bonus for best sales improvement, and I didn't get a red cent for my ideas."

WHAT IT ALL MEANS

All leaders—especially women—need to do the right research before starting the first 100 days to make this critical time pay off. Detailed preparation will help you evaluate the job, set up to do your best work, and understand the role you may need to play in the success of others. The leadership journey is difficult for women because the path is not as well traveled; relationships are trickier to manage, and there are plenty of additional pitfalls along the way. Lucky for all of us, women are willing to ask for directions.

☑ CHAPTER CHECKLIST

- ☐ I understand typical prestart mistakes and how to avoid them.
- ☐ I've done my homework and have recorded my initial impressions (see Accelerator 1B in the Appendix).

All Eyes on You

YOU'VE DONE YOUR homework, you've checked out the organization, and now you have a hint of the challenges ahead. You've evaluated the job, and now it's time to evaluate your capacity to do that job. You need to critically and objectively examine the person you see every day in the mirror.

JUMPSTARTER: *TAKE A GOOD LOOK AT YOURSELF*

Your due diligence should include taking a thoughtful look at who you really are relative to the job you are about to take: your skills, values, fears, quirks, survival instincts, and professional and personal preferences. The higher you climb, the more important a thorough self-analysis will be. If you are facing bigger challenges and taking larger risks, you need all the information you can get before choosing your route. In the first 100 days, you can then develop strategies that exploit your potential, help you establish the smartest first moves, and figure out what else you need. In the long run, it will save you the regret of racing up the mountain only to discover you don't like the view—or getting caught in a completely avoidable crisis.

WHAT'S IMPORTANT TO WOMEN

1. Women have very little room for error. Understanding your capacities and developing appropriate strategies will help you make fewer mistakes.
2. Entering new leadership territory—especially if you are a minority—is scary. Understand your fears so that you can evaluate and manage them.
3. Diversity at the top has a healthy impact on the bottom line. Understanding your personal inventory will help you bring your unique talents, ideas, and perspectives to bear.

Conducting Your Personal Inventory

Don't skim or skip this important activity! It is well worth the mulling time required, even if you've completed similar assessments before. After all, it's well known that we spend 30 percent of our time at the job site, and that doesn't include time for commuting, completing work at home, or brainstorming in the shower. The time you spend now figuring out the right leadership route will pay off for years. At the very least, it will save you months of regret. (See Accelerator 2A in the Appendix for help in conducting a personal assessment.) Think of it as an adventure you can pursue from the comfort of your couch.

Understand Your Abilities and Limitations. By understanding your own skill set and abilities, you can deliberately craft your job in a way that maximizes what you enjoy and do well. For example, Betsy was a successful but mildly dissatisfied consultant. Although her work provided ample financial and intellectual rewards, something was missing. When she accepted a new job at a well-respected newspaper, she took a personal inventory.

INTRODUCING ALLIE

"I've got a career to manage," says Allie whenever she is asked about her latest boyfriend. Single, smart, and extremely driven, her goal to become a CEO is all-consuming. She may not have long to wait.

At 26, Allie is proud to be the youngest regional manager and the only woman in the upper management of a transportation conglomerate. She is rapidly introducing innovative revenue sources for a sluggish line of truck-stop convenience stores. Her success prompted an offer to take over the national territory—a huge leap in responsibility and challenge. The highly visible profit-and-loss work is important to her career goals. It's a great offer, but the potential time bombs are already in place and ticking.

First, despite her top-notch performance, Allie knows that the family-run company is tight-knit. She can travel up a few more rungs until she bumps into the family stronghold—not to mention the glass ceiling. Now may be the time to get that law degree or M.B.A., as she's already been accepted to a first-rate program.

Second, she is being promoted over a 20 year veteran who is male and considered himself a shoe-in for the job. If she takes it, he will be furious and could make her life miserable. He is excellent at the technical side of the work and has some strong strategic relationships, and the company needs his institutional knowledge.

• Allie knows her brainpower and drive help, but her real strengths are her abilities as a creative problem solver and her determination to do whatever a job takes. For example, several years earlier, she personally installed 150 T-1 network lines in the truck-stop convenience stores, saving the company a bundle of money. Her colleagues shook their heads and heated up their caramel lattes while she was busy loading cable and equipment into the back of a com-

(continued)

pany truck. "After all," she said at the time, "I was visiting the stores anyway. Why not go ahead and get it done?"

• Allie loves the idea of leading a cohesive team that is capable of anything. She likes setting a challenging goal, then going for it. Yet she dreads being held accountable for the activities of others—especially that angry jerk who would be reporting to her and would resent her for being a woman.

• For Allie to be her best, she requires the freedom to act and take chances, support from the top, and the ability to get naysayers out of her way. Until now, she has used her skills and smarts to work around calcified attitudes. If she takes the job, she can no longer do end runs around resistant colleagues. She must learn to gain commitment from others and inspire cooperation. Also, she needs quiet space; she doesn't concentrate or perform well in chaos.

• Pondering her darker sides, Allie considers how intensely she reacts when caught in a mistake. As one friend described, "Usually, Allie is all steely composure. There's a disconnect between what you see and what she's actually feeling. Don't play poker with her. In fact, don't even tell her a joke. But if she ever screws up, watch out. She's very tough on herself, and it's not pretty. With that amount of self-criticism, she'll never need a mother-in-law."

When stressed, she becomes remote and distant. People tend to think she is angry and stay clear of her. Allie also measures others by her own high standards. She expects a lot, but it is often tough to know where one stands with her. People tend to stretch to try and prove themselves to her.

She found that she came alive when asked to help managers craft tough conversations because she was fascinated with the psychology required to manage volatile relationships or negotiate around personal agendas. Realizing that, Betsy surreptitiously became an internal coach to high-level managers. Within two years, she landed in the executive suite.

You can also determine which strengths you might overuse. The Center for Creative Leadership has conducted numerous studies on *derailment*—when fast-track, high-achieving managers unexpectedly plateau or get demoted. Surprisingly, the same qualities that are pivotal to a person's rapid rise can hurt their ability to move further. For example, an early-career perfectionist tendency might result in gratuitous overinvolvement and micromanagement later on.

It helps to consider (not obsess over!) your limitations and make plans to mitigate them. A financial whiz with poor speaking skills can take a public-speaking class. Someone who's lousy at details can arrange for administrative help. If you dominate conversations, you can find a trusted ally to signal when you talk too much. You have to understand your limitations before you can manage them.

You may also have skills you take for granted that will contribute to your success. A woman's natural curiosity and willingness to share power and decision-making credit are important traits for managing today's generation of workers.

Making It Work for You

- Learn the results of your job interview from your boss, including where you excelled and any issues that deserve attention. Create a plan to mitigate your weaknesses and take early strategic advantage of your strengths.
- Identify which of your strengths you should demonstrate quickly in your new job, and then find ways to do so. For example, if you are a gifted communicator, you might network externally by speaking to the local civic clubs. Or as an effective collaborator, you might launch early meetings with disenfranchised groups.

- Encourage your boss or predecessor to introduce you by highlighting your skills and how they will contribute to the organization's agenda.
- When meeting your colleagues, describe your prior accomplishments and moments of pride. The enthusiasm you project will be natural, obvious, and contagious. Forget the outdated advice that "it's not nice to brag." Although you may feel uncomfortable at first, self-promotion is a skill that women desperately need to develop. Just don't oversell or overtell—it's boring unless you wrestled alligators or won an Oscar at your last job.
- Evaluate what scares you about leadership, and then determine how to expand your comfort zone. For example, if you fear losing a work-life balance—an issue that many women face—block out chunks of unstructured time. Don't sacrifice that time to schedule creep ("The report took longer than planned. Guess I'll just have to work late again.").
- Think about how the job taps into your personal hopes and dreams. This will help you identify your personal vision for your job.
- Use the answers to these questions to help determine your anchors (see Chapter 3).

Determine What You Need to Be Your Best. Have you considered what circumstances promote your highest level of productivity? Think about the physical setting, the working environment, and the goals and values of the organization. There are probably certain physical conditions and settings in which you thrive. If you don't want your back to the door, plan ahead!

Some women seek a highly charged atmosphere of creative chaos, while others prefer structure, discipline, and order. If you can identify what you need to be your best, you can negotiate for it more effectively. The more you know, the better you can consciously influence the situation. For example, Dena loved the excitement but hated the instability of working in sales. She accepted a government position creating public/private partnerships to support job seekers. Promoting the innovative program combined the thrill and challenge of sales with the job security of a public agency. She led the department's phenomenal growth and solidified its reputation as a premier career-transition center.

Making It Work for You

- Seek ways to create whatever conditions bring out the best in you, be they a high-end monitor, natural lighting, or regular check-in meetings. In Chapter 3, we will discuss how to negotiate for these ideal conditions.

- If the job doesn't provide the physical environment you need, determine how to create it. If, for example, you work in a cubicle and hate interruptions, you might reserve a conference room or set up in the local coffee shop for important phone calls and meetings.

- Discuss your findings with your colleagues. Encourage them to share their own answers to the same questions that you've already asked yourself. Work to create team understanding. For example, if you all need quiet but your workplace sounds like Grand Central at rush hour, you can agree to set "vault hours," when colleagues agree to avoid interrupting one another, or "phones off" times.

You and Your "Shadow." Shadows are your deep-rooted fears, apprehensions, and insecurities. Often buried, they can have a huge impact on how you respond in tough situations. If you avoid the very actions you suspect you need to take, perhaps a shadow is responsible. To recognize and name the fear will allow you to manage it more objectively—and maybe even profit from the lessons it teaches about yourself. The most successful women leaders seldom allow fear to dictate their actions. When there is internal debate, they make the "braver" decision. But first, you have to recognize what fear is holding you back.

For instance, Sally's fast-paced business environment often calls for quick decisions and decisive management. Unfortunately, she prefers a traditionally female, inclusive approach, often taking too long trying to garner support and pound out consensus. Sally may not even recognize her fears of either a challenge to her authority or a power struggle with subordinates. Understanding your root causes of shadows allows you to evaluate their validity and determine how to learn from them. In Sally's case, she could actively develop stronger relationships with people who intimidate her. Or she might encourage productive confrontations as a way to promote healthy debate.

It's useful to examine your automatic responses, particularly under pressure. They are the behaviors that emerge when you are in "survival mode." If you understand your reactions when your back is against the wall, you can learn to mitigate what is not useful. For example, I have been running trails with Erline, a commodities expert, for more than 10 years. We laugh whenever a rabbit startles us, because I always freeze as Erline flees. As a young child, she learned from her five hard-hitting brothers that her best automatic response to danger was to skedaddle. She now makes a conscious effort to stand up for herself and confront domineering management at work. Meanwhile, I must work hard to manage my expressions and respond decisively rather than locking up. During organizational moments of truth—when the atmosphere is tense and the stakes are high— you need to recognize your tendency to control or retreat, to reach out or shut out.

Your intuition is an important source of information. Take time to explore what happens to you physically when you experience red flags—when your subconscious signals that something isn't right. Rather than assume it is the enchilada you had for lunch, you should recognize this as important data. Your tight shoulders or turning stomach can be valuable warning signs. For example, during Cynthia's group interview for a senior management position, her internal alarms went off. Despite the apparent agreement among the panel, something felt wrong. Unable to identify the issue, Cynthia ignored the hunch and accepted the job . . . and now she's miserable. She realized too late that the boss has surrounded himself with yes-men and yes-women, and he undervalues her point of view. So Cynthia feels she has no choice but to restart her job search. Following her intuition would have saved months of frustration if she had worked to figure out the source of her unease.

Making It Work for You

- Ask a trusted colleague or friend to either signal you at the moment or help you role-play when your automatic responses become counterproductive.
- Mentally rehearse responses to challenging situations (such as media assaults, challenging colleagues, attacks on your credentials) before they happen.
- Practice not taking criticism personally. This is an issue that many women face. Allowing your critics to discourage you is a career-limiting move. Don't take the hits. If you do take one, get back up, and forget that you're a girl who is supposed to play nice.
- Keep a list of your nonproductive, high-stress reactions close at hand.
- If you find yourself consistently avoiding a task you know you should complete, think about the underlying fear that may be holding you back.

Understand Your Impact on Others. You can't lead alone, or as a friend of mine says, "You can't be the only one rowing forward."

Your self-analysis process should include learning more about how you affect other people. This determines what you do to bring out the best in your colleagues or how your actions help expand the capacity and commitment of others. Perhaps you tend to challenge the status quo, lead the charge, nurture, or inspire.

Making It Work for You

- Compare what you think your impact is with the perceptions of a close colleague. Pay special attention to differences or surprises.
- Identify what, if any, changes you need to make in your interpersonal interactions. For example, many women tend to treat their own conversational topics as "tentative" and work hard to support and pursue others' topics. See if you can maintain your innate sensitivity to the conversational needs of others without sacrificing attention to your own issues.
- Think about how you can tap into the best of your leadership style to bring focus and cohesion to your team.
- See Chapter 4 for ideas on launching your first team meetings.
- See Chapter 7 for ideas on managing tough challenges with individuals and your team.

Understand Your Issues Versus Others' Projections. The clearer you are about your own style and quirks, the easier it is to interpret what is projected onto you. Let's say that you receive feedback portraying you as overbearing, which is how many strong women, fairly or not, are classified. If your self-assessment and conversations with colleagues contradict such a picture, think twice. Part of the new feedback may be about you, but the rest may be associated with your status as the first woman in your position. Knowing your approach and effect on others makes it easier to sort out the root of the issue and possible solutions.

For example, Allie, the young business prodigy, is rapidly creating innovative revenue sources for a sluggish line of truck stops. By doing so, she is also eclipsing older and more experienced men on her way to senior management. The resentment is growing. Allie must work hard to determine whether she plays a role in any interpersonal breakdown, or if being young, successful, and female is the primary reason for the tension. She needs to understand which part of the relationship problem is hers to fix.

Making it Work for You

- If you know yourself well and can quickly assess what is triggering a negative situation, you don't have to waste time worrying about other people's problems. Instead, you can read the cues and take appropriate action.
- When you do receive feedback about a personal limitation, you won't be caught by surprise or feel compelled to defend yourself. You can quickly take responsibility and move on to finding solutions.

JUMPSTARTER: *WHO-YOU-ARE-IS-WHAT-THEY-NEED AUTHENTICITY*

You must be able to bring your whole self into your leadership role. Otherwise, it's one-dimensional leadership and unsustainable—like a wall with only one support. I have to be able to admit I make mistakes sometimes.

—Community media executive

LIN'S PERSONAL INVENTORY

In preparing for her switch from human resources to supervisor of a technical department, Lin answered the questions that intrigued her in Accelerator 2A (see the Appendix) and discovered the following:

- **Past and present:** Lin is proudest of the moments when her effective coaching transformed an underperforming employee. She loves to help people maximize their contributions and enjoy their work. She believes work should be fun and rewarding, and she thrives when people acknowledge her own contributions.

- **Her strengths:** She is respectful, detail-oriented, technically competent, an effective communicator (if the news is good), willing to share credit, an excellent listener, and consistent with follow-through. Finally, she has an incredible sense of humor that has saved her in dicey spots more often that she might like to admit.

- **Where she needs to improve:** Lin tends to promise and take on too much, a typical trait in women. She sometimes fails to set clear boundaries in professional relationships. Although she is good with details, she is sometimes obsessive. She tends to give away credit that is rightfully hers—another common characteristic in women executives. She can get caught up in her need to be right in any argument, which causes others to verbally concede while silently maintaining their own viewpoints.

- **What attracts her to this job:** She enjoys the creative challenge and authority, but she primarily needs the money the promotion will provide. As a single parent with two kids, she needs to earn as much as possible.

- **What scares her about this promotion:** Lin is comfortable with confrontation and knows that her new job will be filled with showdowns. However, she is very uncomfortable with unspoken, covert tension.

She is also concerned about work-life stress, which is an issue that confronts many working mothers. When she's at home, she thinks she should be working, and when she's working late, she worries about the time away from her children.

• **Hopes and dreams:** Lin wants to break out of the human resources career path. The skills she gains from guiding the company through software integration, collaborating across technology fiefdoms, and managing a multimillion-dollar project will help her accomplish that. She also wants to continue creating family milestones. Lin is the only member of her family to graduate from college; and she wants to rise higher in the organization than anyone thought possible.

• **To be her best:** Lin must feel at peace both at the office and at home. She needs to reconcile her fixation on productivity with the demands of a lifestyle that focuses on both work and family. Lin also needs to feel that she is providing a service that others value.

• **A quirk that needs work:** Lin encourages an open-door policy. However, she bristles if someone knocks or enters when she shuts her door.

• **A dilemma:** Lin likes public service, but she hates the slow progress and inflexible attitudes that accompany such work. She is hoping that as a leader, she will be able to instill excitement and a desire for progress in her staff.

• **Her shadows:** When under extreme stress, Lin gets red in the face and locks her jaw. Her body language becomes stiff and rigid—a trait she detests in others. She becomes overly focused and can alienate those who are accustomed to her good nature and raucous humor. Worse, she takes trouble home and is unnecessarily tough on her kids as a result.

• **Impact she has on others:** Lin shows limitless confidence in other people she trusts. She is not afraid to delegate and is willing to share credit for excellent work. People like working under her leadership and want to do a good job for her.

It takes a paragraph to write and perhaps years to achieve, but feeling comfortable in your own skin will promote your leadership credibility and increase your value to any organization. Part of taking a good look at yourself is to consider what conditions help you achieve authenticity—being true to yourself. It may sound a little corny, but it's still critical.

My brother once quipped as he left to change out of his business suit, "This suit is my image, but not my comfort." Who wouldn't trade a tie for a T-shirt? His unspoken message was far more powerful. He was working in an organization that had recently been acquired and was planning layoffs of middle management. It's tough to be authentic when the doom that's looming could be your own. Besides, who wants to always feel like they are on parade?

Consider the circumstances that encourage or prevent you from injecting your whole self into your leadership role. It may be the actions or attitudes of your colleagues; the values of your department (for example, the emphasis on individual competition instead of collaboration); your level of control; or, as in my brother's case, the business context. Women especially need to tap into these feelings to lead effectively. Once you understand what helps you feel comfortable and authentic, you can actively take on your role and hit the ground running.

For example, Kris was in the military for 10 years. She felt forced to rein in her outgoing personality to head off verbal and physical advances from male colleagues. Gradually, she was given the nickname "The Ironclad Bitch," and her career stalled. She realized her exit was overdue when she slammed a fellow serviceman against the wall and said, "Don't *ever* call me honey again!" By not taking a personal inventory as she moved up the ranks, Kris missed the chance to consider what she needed to be authentic. She did not set clear, firm guidelines with other officers about their interactions and therefore suffered a tough few years. She is now a popular consultant, and her laughter echoes through the halls of her organization.

Making It Work for You

- Women who succumb to pressure to act out of sync with who they are will prematurely plateau in their careers. Be who you are, flaws and all.
- Though the universal tug is to become one of the crowd, your real value comes in being unique within the group.
- When you know what contributes to your ability to be authentic, you can actively create those circumstances.

INTRODUCING ELAINE

Elaine is a successful department head at a large health care system. There are plenty of financial and intellectual rewards, but she tires of corporate mandates that are counterproductive to good medicine and public service. She has been offered the hospital administrator position at a small community hospital. She loves the idea of being active in a community and enjoying a direct link to the board.

Since she's married with two high school–age kids, the move will be disruptive. Her husband, a writer, is mobile, but her children will take the biggest hit socially and psychologically, and as a mother, this is something she takes very seriously. Elaine needs to think things over. Is this job going to be worth the stress on her family? If she is successful, she believes it will be the right choice

(continued)

in the long run. But what will it take to be successful? It's time to figure that out.

Elaine is a financial whiz and a gifted communicator and negotiator. She is a master at crafting her message, and she's a spin doctor with integrity. As a strategist, Elaine often uses her communication skills to convince people to adopt long-range goals that may require short-term pain.

For example, early in her career, she informed the director of nutrition that the hospital would save more than 40 percent by contracting out food services, placing his job at risk. But after Elaine finessed the meeting, he walked out thanking her and eager to help make the transition work.

"She could tell you to go to hell and you'd walk away whistling," her secretary says with a laugh. "I've overheard her do that time and again."

Elaine is proud of her ability to engage people and groups in productive conversation. In earlier assignments, she was effective both at implementing a radical new performance management system and at convincing "old-timers" to get on board with technology. She deftly moves individuals away from polarized positions and into joint problem solving.

Her skills would certainly be tested in the administrator's job. The hospital is in financial trouble, and employee morale is at an all-time low. She would have her work cut out for her, which reminds her of something else—she's a workaholic.

She would have to control her work habits while her family made the transition. Like many women, Elaine would be torn between the demands of the job and the strong need to help her kids. "They don't really confide in me, but I know they want me around," she says. "In fact, I'll bet they want me to ask questions, whether they answer them or not. If nothing else, they need someone to roll their eyes at."

Thinking about her dark side, Elaine feels exposure. She shudders at the thought that people might decide she isn't cut out to lead. She tends to play down her mistakes. Her parents were substance abusers, and Elaine learned early how to stay under the radar and shift blame. She deeply fears "getting caught"—whatever that means.

By the way, when my brother eventually received his dismissal notice, he opened a pizza franchise and now owns nearly 30 stores. His professional attire? Sweat suits.

WHAT IT ALL MEANS

If you take a good look at yourself once you understand your new position, you can evaluate the job, set up to do your best work, and understand the role you'll play in others' success. It prepares you both physically and mentally, then allows you to begin developing strategies for taking charge of your start. You'll know what you need to plan and negotiate to maximize your success.

☑ CHAPTER CHECKLIST

- ☐ I know my leadership strengths and challenges as they relate to this job.
- ☐ I know the working conditions that will contribute to my optimal performance in my new position.
- ☐ I understand the impact I typically have on others.
- ☐ I understand my automatic, instinctive responses.
- ☐ I know what I need to be authentic in my leadership role.

CHAPTER 3

Your Going-In Strategy

YOU'VE DONE YOUR homework by taking a good look at both the organization and yourself. Now it's time to discuss what you should learn, negotiate, question, and plan. The period between accepting the position and your first day on the job is a fantastic opportunity—take advantage of it. By the time you start work, you need to have access to important answers and should be capable of conducting critical negotiations to set the stage for accelerating your success.

In this chapter, you will create a *going-in strategy*, which means developing an entry plan, identifying your leadership anchors, constructing a fail-safe support system, appropriately communicating your needs, and making sure you can leave the door open for further negotiation.

JUMPSTARTER: *DEVELOP AN ENTRY PLAN*

Ever notice that some companies have exit strategies, but no entry strategies? It amazes me how many otherwise enlightened organizations will have a well-developed timetable for retirement, but no clear plan for new leaders' incoming transitions. As leadership transition expert Tom Adams wrote in the article "Leadership Transitions: Critical Thresholds" published in *Nonprofit Quarterly*, without such a plan, you will be "at risk of arbitrary and changing expectations, unfair evaluation, and perhaps even dismissal."

In fact, fewer than 30 percent of companies have well-constructed plans for incorporating new executives. Yet research shows that a carefully considered beginning is an important contribution to a leader's ultimate success. So you should quite legitimately jump the gun by working with your board or boss to develop a clear blueprint for your first 100 days. This blueprint will serve as both a valuable tool and an early indicator of the potential quality of your relationship. A work plan will help you avoid fallout from conflict at the board level, a boss's whims, and ultimately a lousy evaluation.

If your boss or board hesitates to help create the plan, it's a potential red flag. After all, if they don't much care how you start, they may care even less about how (or when or if) you finish. Develop your plan anyway—it's going to be useful later.

Here are the critical points that should form the basis for any entry plan. You should always feel free to add other points and ask other questions, but this list will serve as a solid foundation (see Accelerator 3A in the Appendix).

• **Expectations:** Learn exactly what your employer expects of you—both for the first 100 days and for your first year—in terms of performance, relationships, and concrete results.

• **Communication:** First, learn from your boss or interview panelist why you were chosen and any development information that was gathered during the selection process. Determine how and when you'll be able to check in to monitor your progress. By the same token, if you are going to lead others who were candidates for your job, make sure your boss lets them know why they were not chosen.

Next, insist that the organization announce both the leadership change and any predetermined strategy. If a major change
is pending (especially if it's unpopular), your boss should emphasize that the decision is made and that you were specifically
selected to help make that change successful. This way, your
coworkers will see you more as the person whose role is to help
them adapt rather than as the interloper trying to shake things
up. You're the mechanic that's going to keep the car running,
not the car dealer trying to sell them on spinning hubcaps and
extra undercoating. Get clear agreement that top management
will both publicly and privately support you.

Finally, secure a regular check-in time with your boss, as well
as arrangements for getting immediate, honest feedback.

• **Understanding:** Make sure that everyone's on the same
page regarding key strategic issues and your roles and responsibilities. If you and your boss don't agree on strategy and direction, brace yourself for a challenging start. Either sharpen up
your persuasion skills, or pull out your résumé.

• **Evaluating progress:** Give yourself a baseline of comprehensive first impressions. Remember to use the chart found
in Accelerator 1B. You'll eventually compare what you think
you know versus what you discover to be true later in your first
100 days.

• **Your support system:** Determine the support you will
need, then create the necessary agreements with your boss for
getting it. (Support systems will be discussed in detail later in
this chapter.) If you are new to the company, consider negotiating for an assigned mentor or group of advisors who can guide
you safely past any organizational or cultural land mines.

For example, years ago, on a kayak expedition in the South
Seas, I landed in exhaustion on a remote beach next to an island
village. Befriending a gracious English-speaking native, I asked

him to guide me to the chief, then translate my request for permission to camp. As we strolled along the white sands, the sun emerged from a cloudy sky and began to scorch. Pulling off my windbreaker, I tossed it over my shoulder, thumb in collar. My aghast host frantically motioned me to snatch the coat off my shoulder. My gesture was a shocking show of disrespect to the approaching chief—a serious cultural land mine. It could have easily resulted in a firm "No, you are not welcome here" and another 20 miles of paddling.

JUMPSTARTER: *IDENTIFY YOUR LEADERSHIP ANCHORS*

> If I hadn't developed my anchors, I could never have faced the challenges to my strategy from senior staff members.
>
> —Budget analyst, city agency

Once you've established an entry plan, your next task is to develop your leadership anchors. *Anchors* are the rules of engagement that govern your leadership style. For some, an anchor is a personal vision, ambition, or mission. Others focus on values and behaviors that support them. In this section, you will determine exactly what your anchors are. In later chapters, we will explain how to use these anchors to create a foundation, build credibility, develop your team, and face organizational moments of truth.

Anchors as Personal Vision

For some, the principal anchor is their personal sense of purpose—an individual mission (like making a positive difference) or the mission of the organization. Living in congruence with your purpose gives you the courage to do what's necessary without second-guessing yourself. Anchors can also be a set of personal values and guiding principles that govern daily interaction.

For example, Beth recently took charge of a large food bank in the Pacific Northwest. The nonprofit organization was in financial crisis, forcing her to make some draconian decisions. The layoffs and operational changes caused incredible pain and nervousness among the employees. When I asked her, in the midst of all the uncertainty, whether she was having trouble sleeping at night, she simply replied, "No, because I am doing what matters—finding the best way to feed hungry people." That is her personal vision.

Anchors as Codes of Conduct

Anchors can be an explicit set of behaviors. They emerge from values and principles, but they are communicated as codes of conduct. Let's say that you value efficiency. Your resulting anchors might be as follows:

- Look for ways to save time, conserve resources, or eliminate unnecessary steps.
- Take the time to get it right the first time.

LIN'S ANCHORS

Impatient with unresolved conflict, Lin's first anchor is: "If you have a problem, go to the source." Coming from a close-knit family, she was taught from an early age that no matter what happened at home, the family provides a united front to the world. This formed the basis for her second anchor: "Our issues are our own; we will give seamless service to the customer."

If you particularly value respect, you may believe that staff should fault plans rather than people or that you want to deal with conflict directly—no indirect complaints.

Additional examples of anchors as codes of conduct include the following:

- I told my staff to never, under any circumstances, lie to me.
- What is said here, stays here. We will present a united front to our external customers.
- We have to have fun here.
- If we say we will get it done, we will get it done. If we say we have a deadline, we meet the deadline.

Your anchors are nonnegotiable. If you suspect an organization will pressure you to act contrary to your anchors, you must seriously consider whether it is worth the stress and challenge. Many of the decisions you make as a leader are, of course, situational responses to strategic initiatives, performance, context, and market conditions. Your anchors should never be subject to these variables.

Don't think of anchors as simply a buzzword. They are your leadership DNA and are as unalterable as your shoe size. If you ruled the world and faced no consequences for your actions, you would still live by them. Remember, we're trying to help you identify and develop your anchors, not invent them. You already have a hardwired set of guiding principles. The process of thinking about, articulating, and living by those principles will ultimately focus your energies and increase your confidence.

You can't change your anchors, and you shouldn't profess to have a particular anchor just because it sounds appealing. If you claim to operate with an anchor that spins well but does not reflect who you really are, you'll eventually be under stress and act out of sync with that anchor—and then you can kiss your credibility good-bye. You don't want to end up as the professional equivalent of the televangelist caught having an illicit affair.

Why Develop Anchors?

Having anchors gave me the strength to make very painful personnel decisions.

—Executive director, nonprofit agency

In later chapters, we will discuss how to use anchors during critical stages in your first 100 days. But before we talk about how to use your anchors, you need to understand why they're so important. Why should you spend so much time learning about them?

To Create First Connections. When you haven't had time to sort out the strategic and operational priorities, communicating your anchors settles apprehension and inspires confidence. Your key stakeholders can move from considering you an unknown wild card to envisioning what their world will be like under your leadership.

For example, at her first meeting, an elected official told her team, "I will support you all the way, if you are honest and do your best to serve our constituents." She did not yet know their strategic direction or her agenda, but it was a good framework for beginning their work together.

To Give You Strength. When your project is in crisis, working in agreement with your anchors will give you the strength and courage to do what's needed. Knowing, communicating, and acting on your anchors will help you land on your feet, no matter how slippery the slope.

> ## ALLIE'S ANCHORS
>
> A history buff, Allie is fascinated with Napoleon Bonaparte. Two quotes attributed to him really resonate for her: "If you say you're going to take Vienna, take Vienna," and "It is better to have a known enemy than a forced ally." She considers those lines as she writes her own anchors: "We will do what it takes to get the job done," and "Be who you will, be what you will, but be honest."

To Build Credibility. To act authentically and in accordance with your anchors solidifies your credibility and increases the trust others have in you. Conversely, if you are pressured to act against what is important, your personal stress level will increase even as you lose standing across the board.

For example, Carrie's new boss encouraged risk taking, so she took him at his word. Her first effort was an embarrassing failure. However, her boss responded to her bleak report with, "That's not so bad. Let's see how we can move this forward." Imagine her relief, appreciation, and loyalty. She would work for him in a snake pit.

To Help Develop Your Team. Teams can go through stages of development ranging from superficiality to the precision orchestration of a symphony. In Chapter 7, we will discuss how you can use your anchors to help accelerate a team's evolution.

Making It Work for You

- **The development of anchors is an important step for all leaders.** However, since women face more scrutiny and a narrower band of permissible approaches, using anchors will provide an additional source of strength and personal resolve when pressure builds.

ELAINE'S ANCHORS

Her Southern upbringing probably led to Elaine's anchors. She strongly believes that mutual respect is the proper foundation for any work environment. When she takes over hospital administration and launches tough negotiations to save the hospital, she will insist that disagreements be discussed respectfully.

- **Your anchor message should be crafted with your audience in mind.** A scrappy fire chief once said, "My key anchor is that I don't pay people to sleep." The message is clear, but it probably received a mixed reception—or even sparked a minor rebellion due to its bluntness.

In Chapter 5, we will provide ideas for communicating all your messages successfully. Turn to Accelerator 3B in the Appendix for more help identifying your anchors.

JUMPSTARTER: *CREATE A FAIL-SAFE SUPPORT SYSTEM*

Leadership comes with emotional, psychological, and even physical price tags. Be sure to get the support you need, be it family time, regular gym workouts, a mentor, or the boss's backing. You must perform an honest assessment about the help you are going to need as you lead others. Then, you should feel good about creating the space to get it.

In conversations with hundreds of executives, the overwhelming majority said they should have taken better care of themselves to maintain health, relationships, stamina, and spirit. They somehow expected to sustain the energy of their organizations without replenishing their own.

WHAT'S IMPORTANT TO WOMEN

- With the overwhelming demands on a new executive's time, women tend to sacrifice their self-care and well-being. It's lousy business to miss out on the obvious benefits of a workable support system.
- With less free time, the demands of multiple roles, and the pressures of being different, it's critical for women leaders to vent, relax, and recharge.
- Women historically have not received the clubby advice available in the men's locker room or on the golf course. They must be proactive about finding mentors and other kinds of professional support.
- Many new female leaders have little experience enduring hard-hitting business tactics. They periodically need to escape the fray.

Social/Emotional

Reconnecting outward means regaining hope and feeling free to be completely vulnerable. When the unions are preparing to strike, your direct reports are angry, or your most lucrative client leaves, you need a safe place to fall apart, pull together, and restart.

Spiritual

Reconnecting inward (or upward) means replenishing your soul. This includes seeking those circumstances that make you feel truly contented. Such a circumstance might be a place—for example, a rustic retreat—or an activity—prayer, meditation, painting, gardening, and so forth. These are the places and moments when you feel connected to and invigorated by inner resources that give you strength.

Physical

Diet, sleep, and exercise—all the mundane machinery of keeping yourself in top condition. Give yourself time and permission to hit the gym, eat a decent meal, or get to bed on time. Consider your exercise times just as sacred as your staff meetings. If the gym is too far, dust off that home workout equipment and find a new place to hang your laundry.

Professional

A variety of resources can help you enhance and supplement your on-the-job abilities, both inside and outside your organization.

- **Professional associations:** Surf the Internet or talk to colleagues to find information on local chapters, meetings, and events.
- **Informal mentors:** Contact people you admire and ask them for advice to aid in your transitions or other critical times.
- **Formal mentoring programs:** Many organizations offer on-the-job mentoring programs. Your human resources contacts may be able to help.
- **Professional coaching:** The coaching industry is growing at about 40 percent a year. Look for someone with the following characteristics:
  - Is likeable and trustworthy
  - Believes in your potential
  - Can be honest without reprimanding you
  - Allows you to be vulnerable
  - Asks the tough questions
  - Makes you analyze your basic assumptions

Think about the additional personal resources you need— emotionally, spiritually, physically, and professionally. Negotiate

LIN'S SUPPORT SYSTEM

Lin needs her boss to back her up because the upcoming changes will be unpopular with some of her staff. Until now, the information technology group has enjoyed free reign when purchasing software. The requirement for improved integration will necessitate a coordinated, collaborative relationship—the equivalent of asking the Hatfields to room with the McCoys. All sides will be quick to complain to the boss.

She must insist on her boss's backup, which means he must agree to the following:

- Tell staff to support Lin's decisions
- Include Lin in any conversations or complaints about her leadership
- Insist that Lin's decisions are final and nonnegotiable whenever he is absent

In addition, Lin needs to plan to meet every other week for lunch with buddies from school. They are always good for laughs, and she's going to need her sense of humor over the next few months. Just hearing about her friend Marsha's ongoing saga with a backbiting, boss-seducing, credit-stealing cohort puts Lin's challenges into amusing perspective.

for these resources early in your tenure. Use the chart in Accelerator 3C to help you organize your needs.

JUMPSTARTER: *PLAN YOUR FIRST NEGOTIATIONS*

If only I could collect a dollar from every female leader who moaned, "I wish I could renegotiate." Assume everything is up for negotiation until you learn otherwise. If your employer is smart, he or she will understand your desire to review options and negotiate all aspects of your position. Perhaps you want a different benefits package, the freedom to volunteer at your child's school, or more autonomy with the budget. Asking is obviously no guarantee that you'll get what you want, but not asking does guarantee that you won't get what you want.

A second prestart item is the establishment of your working relationship with the board and your boss. Pay particular attention to the parameters and boundaries:

- Clear roles and responsibilities
- The extent of their authority related to your work (Don't wait for a personnel crisis to discover that board members think they have control over your day-to-day management.)

For example, Mary, a CEO at a successful nonprofit, was appalled when a board member who specialized in public relations told her not to provide a television interview. "I've been giving presentations for 20 years," she fumed. "How can she tell me not to do this?" More critical questions are "What authority does Mary's board have?" and "Is it the board's responsibility to make these decisions?"

Replacing a Founder

This can be very tricky, especially if he or she retains a majority share or continuing interest in the company. Negotiate this challenge to your authority early and very carefully. The founder's "gone fishing" attitude lasts a couple of weeks, then he or she gets bored or worried, and suddenly you have an uninvited expert looking over your shoulder. Staff, through habit, will seek direction from this lingering eminence. Your founder must have a well-planned exit strategy, which should be communicated across the company. Before you begin, clarify the lines of decision making and authority, and decide together how you as the successor can best serve the organization. The founder may choose to become a trusted advisor or part-time manager. However, founders often serve best if they just leave—and stay gone.

Women in Negotiations

You get what you tolerate.

—Susan Scott, *Fierce Conversations*

Your leadership transition is a great time to bargain for vital resources: time, money, additional developmental support, feedback, scope, and boundaries. You must be prepared to haggle for what you need. Unfortunately, this is an area where women typically struggle. They limit themselves during this phase in several different ways.

Women Don't Recognize the Opportunity to Negotiate. In their wonderful book *Women Don't Ask*, Linda Babcock and Sara Laschever described the tendency of women to accept a first offer, failing to recognize the opportunity for negotiation. They are afraid or reluctant to ask for what they need. Several well-established executive women I interviewed did not negotiate before taking a position. They said, "I wanted the job; what was I supposed to do? If I argued too much, they might have withdrawn the offer."

For example, while in college, Betsy, who just sold her very successful consulting practice, learned to bargain for a car. After a tedious negotiation, the salesman quoted a "final" figure and told her to take it or leave it. Betsy went home to figure out her finances and told her dad she had made a deal. Her father quietly said, "Betsy, why don't you make a $500 phone call?" encouraging her to make one more offer. Reluctantly, Betsy made the call. Sure enough, the salesman agreed to her price.

Are there "$500 phone calls"—or meetings or interviews—you can make? Perhaps your salary is set, but you can negotiate for flextime or telecommuting days. For example, organizers of a convention asked Mary Beth, a popular travel writer, to give a speech, but they could not afford her usual fee. Mary Beth accepted the arrangement by negotiating in-kind payments of free travel and accommodations in a luxurious Napa Valley spa.

Women Back Down. Women are more relationship-focused than men, who find comfort in hierarchy and rank. When the negotiations get heated and the relationship appears to be at risk, women may be more likely than men to back down.

Women Put Others First. Women are nurturers, usually putting children, parents, friends, and other loved ones first. By providing for others, they are more likely to settle for less for themselves.

Women Suffer from Superwoman Syndrome. Women often have to work harder to get what they need and get ahead. They may tend to take on too much without insisting on more support. For example, when Laura took over the supervision of a busy communications center, she knew it was a big job. The position had not been filled for a number of years. In the first year, she was expected to learn the job at floor level, supervise three shifts, create a training plan, and be responsible for all administrative duties associated with the division. She felt she had to do it all. After three months, the skip left her step. In six months, she was chronically tired. After nine months, she was burned out and so perpetually grumpy that she made Oscar the Grouch seem like Cinderella's Fairy Godmother.

A Woman's Guide to Negotiation

First, **enter negotiations with a plan.** Clearly outline your ideal scenario and what you need to achieve it. Consider the "must-

---

LIN TAKES IT EASY

Lin remembers from her self-assessment that she tends to take on too much. During the recruiting phase, she learns that a major process improvement project is under way. If she joins the committees, she will quickly learn the work and develop some key partnerships with other staff. However, knowing her tendency to overcommit, Lin asks to observe (not formally join) the committee meetings instead. Once she has completed her transition, she will sign up for only those committees that are a good use of her time.

---

haves" that are nonnegotiable, the "should-haves" that you can discuss, and the "nice-to-haves" that you would be willing to sacrifice. Be prepared to dig in and fight when your must-haves—the deal breakers—are at stake. Use the tool provided in Accelerator 3D to keep your priorities clear.

Next, **clearly articulate what you need and why.** When you express your interest or the "why" in negotiations, the potential for innovative solutions increases.

Negotiations should focus on resolving competing interests. Additional personnel may not be in the budget, but perhaps you can negotiate the ability to hire a consulting firm. Flexible working hours may be impossible for the organization, but a 4-day, 10-hour work schedule may meet your needs for family time. Articulating the rationale for your requests will lead to more creative ways to satisfy both you and the organization.

Keep Your Cool. Your personal interactions in this phase are often an accurate predictor of how things will proceed. As the negotiation goes, so goes the contract. It's important that you be polite and respectful, but firm. Disagree agreeably, but stand up

WHAT ALLIE NEEDS

Allie's job will require her to improve revenue by $10 million in her first year—a 15 percent increase. She knows she can institute systems to prevent staff pilfering, but she is unsure of the potential savings. She will take the first couple of months to learn more. If upgrading the internal systems doesn't produce the anticipated results, she may need additional resources, like advertising or promotional budgets, to make up the difference. She also knows that the new policies will anger employees and create complaints about her management. Therefore, Allie's must-haves are the ability to negotiate for additional resources and backup from her boss when the inevitable grumbling about the new systems begins.

for yourself. Remember, you are negotiating so that you can provide your employer with your best work.

For example, Maggie, the CEO of a large insurance conglomerate, has a "smiling reputation." Her high-level antagonists, who are elected officials, say that her smile is an indicator that she will not budge from her position.

Avoid Making Promises You Can't Keep. In your eagerness to make a great impression, don't make promises you can't keep. Don't wait until you are signed on to find out it would take a battalion to accomplish what is expected of you. Pay particular attention to any requirements that rely heavily on variables beyond your control.

Communicate What You Need to Be Successful. You know what it takes for you to work at your highest potential (refer back to your answers in Accelerator 2A). Convey those needs. This goes beyond the standard terms of employment and finances to

---

WHAT LIN NEEDS

Lin, a single parent, can work long days when her mother is available to help with the children. However, she must be able to respond to school emergencies and other child-related issues. Remembering that her kids' well-being is an important requirement for her to do her best work, Lin must negotiate for scheduling flexibility.

---

include the working atmosphere or kind of relationship you want with your boss or colleagues. Communicate implicitly by modeling your values. Be explicit by openly discussing what you value in a work setting and relationships with your colleagues.

Leave the Door Open to Further Negotiations. Before you start the job—even if you are being promoted in an organization you're familiar with—you cannot know everything. You will be making some agreements based on a (hopefully shared) set of assumptions. Articulate what those assumptions are, and be clear that if you discover a different set of circumstances, you may need to renegotiate for additional resources. This is very important if you are inheriting a major change initiative.

For example, Jan is a fire chief in the Midwest. During her budget presentations to the city council, she alerted them of possible future requests. For example, in 2004, she said, "I want to remind you that I am not asking for additional personnel this year. The time may come, however, when I will need to make that request."

WHAT IT ALL MEANS

By now, all the pieces of your transition puzzle are firmly in place. You should have a solid going-in strategy, the strength pro-

WHAT ELAINE NEEDS

One of Elaine's first tasks will be tough wage bargaining with multiple unions. Her predecessor typically used hardball tactics during contract negotiations. Although often successful in the short term, the unions have become disenfranchised and embittered in recent years. As the work pool for health care employees shrinks, Elaine knows her hospital must improve relations between management and employees. One important step will be to introduce the interest-based approach in negotiations, which promotes common understanding, collaboration, and honest dialogue. She also wants to avoid reaching a tentative agreement, only to have it negated by her board. She will negotiate for clear lines of authority, especially in bargaining, before she starts the job.

vided by your anchors and support systems, and an opportunity for continuing negotiations throughout your transition period. We'll plan your first impression in Chapter 4, and then you'll be ready to launch your first 100 days.

☑ CHAPTER CHECKLIST

- ☐ I have developed an entry plan.
- ☐ I have identified my leadership anchors.
- ☐ I have a strong support system in place.
- ☐ I have communicated what I need to be successful.
- ☐ I have negotiated for the appropriate conditions and resources, and I have kept the door open for future negotiations as circumstances require.

CHAPTER

Day One

THE FIRST 100 days of a new leadership position are as charged with possibility as the pause between a flash of lightning and the following clap of thunder. You have everyone's attention, and you should use it to establish first-rate communication.

That's easy to say, but too often the requirements of learning the job, absorbing data, and getting acquainted with colleagues take top priority. New leaders who fail to plan and manage their message are missing a terrific opportunity. From the moment you discuss a potential new job, good communication is a *sine qua non*—and it involves far more than a few well-written memos and pithy speeches.

To be effective, you need to manage your message well, both before you start the job and as it evolves throughout your first 100 days. We'll talk more about your communication plan and accompanying challenges after you take over. During your first few days, your priority will be to meet with your executive team and other key players to accomplish the following:

- Manage your first impression
- Set the tone by communicating your leadership anchors

- Communicate your preferred leadership style
- Begin to verify operational issues (You will already have a hypothesis.)
- Get to know key people
- Communicate and get feedback on your plan of entry

JUMPSTARTER: *PROACTIVELY MANAGE YOUR FIRST IMPRESSION*

You have a working hypothesis for your job and the organization. You have also conducted a personal inventory about your leadership style and preferences. Based on what you know so far, decide what your leadership first impression should be. What are the leadership messages you need to convey? Perhaps you need to project your no-nonsense, direct style. Conversely, maybe you want to demonstrate that you are an accessible team player. It's much easier to establish a reputation than to change it later, so plan ahead.

You Are in the First-Impression Business

First impressions last forever. For example, researchers from Harvard asked raters to watch six-second, silent video clips of college instructors. In that brief footage, they could predict who would receive the highest ratings from students at the end of the semester. In other words, in the time it took to read this paragraph, a first impression could be formed and irrevocably sealed. In fact, others may already have their first impression of you before you even show up.

For example, I recently attended a networking luncheon with a successful marketing consultant. Prior to her arrival, several people there spoke enthusiastically about her excellent and well-earned reputation. Before the sorbet was served, she had landed two lucrative contracts. I doubt it was luck; I suspect she placed a couple of well-timed phone calls to her "client fans" prior to the meal. The third-person referral was planned before she entered the room, and her positive first impression preceded her arrival.

Perception Becomes Reality

Plenty of research proves that perception can influence outcome. For example, there are numerous studies proving that when a teacher is erroneously informed that certain students are gifted, the teacher's "objective" evaluation of their performance dramatically improves. At Harvard, random students were told they had "gifted" pet rats. The so-called smarter rodents actually performed better in maze competitions—perhaps urged on and better trained by the students' higher expectations and more relaxed training. Think of the implications for your kids, your dog, and yourself. If the word gets out that you are a winner, you will, indeed, become a winner.

It happens like this:

- **Expectations and impressions are formed, logically or not.** Sarah hears through the corporate rumor mill that her new boss, Jane, is cold and unapproachable.
- **Expectations are communicated with overt and subtle behaviors.** Sarah, typically a jovial cutup, tones down the clowning when she meets Jane. Sarah may also unconsciously look for behaviors that confirm her first impression. Jane doesn't smile much, so Sarah concludes she has no sense of humor.
- **The behaviors brought about by these expectations cause, in turn, a response or behavioral adjustment.** Jane notices Sarah is less friendly with her than she is with others. She unconsciously holds back and keeps her mood detached and serious in Sarah's presence.
- **The original perception becomes essentially true.** Jane and Sarah's behavior toward each other remains cold and formal.

You Are in a Fishbowl

While you are trying to get established, others are trying to figure you out. Every choice reverberates. Even if you are a promoted old-timer, people are watching you from a new angle and making decisions about your attitude, competence, and relationships. Every detail seems fraught with implications:

- Why is she having lunch with that person? Why did she go out to a restaurant when our last boss always ate at the company café?
- Why is her door closed?
- Why is she interviewing that department first?
- What's our relationship going to be now that she's a head honcho?
- Why was her first meeting with so-and-so an hour, when mine was only 35 minutes?

Like it or not, consciously or not, you are always communicating.

WHAT'S IMPORTANT TO WOMEN

Women in male-dominated fields should pay particular attention to managing the first impression. A new female leader may have to battle gender prejudice that has nothing to do with her skills and qualifications. Despite her talent and drive, she may have to prove herself again and again. In fact, research shows that we often discount or ignore information that runs contrary to previously formed opinions. If prejudice exists about a woman's ability to lead, it is very difficult to change. Managing your own first impression is the first strike at dispelling negative preconceptions. Like a white rapper or a short basketball player, you will have to earn your credibility.

Plan Ahead

Stepping into a sandbox of white flour, your first footprint will scatter thousands of particles in many directions—which is exactly how communication often travels in organizations. You don't need the red designer outfit, but you do need to look for creative ways to start strong, especially if you expect to enter a challenging situation. Here are some examples of seizing the initiative:

- You are replacing a popular leader. You might attend key meetings together and have him or her praise you publicly.
- You are expected to rally a polarized group. Get the word out via your new boss that you are a strong team player and expect the same from others.
- You are taking over a nonprofit with large funding needs. Get your picture and a complimentary write-up in front of potential donors as quickly as possible. Don't underestimate the power of the third-party endorsement.

ALLIE PLANS HER START

Allie will be supervising Dave, a longtime employee who was passed up for her job. She knows that he resents her and will try to undermine her leadership. Allie should encourage her new boss to meet with Dave before she begins to explain why Dave was not selected for the position, and to clarify that Dave is an important asset to the team and will be expected to support Allie's leadership. He should reiterate to Dave that Allie is a top performer.

Ideas for Managing First Impressions

- Ask your boss to send an announcement letter that articulates how your unique strengths will benefit the organization.
- Ask popular individuals to give you an informal tour and introduce you around.
- Capitalize on informal opportunities to participate in conversations. Connect as both a person and a position.
- Plan activities that will project your desired image. For example, if prior leadership was labeled inaccessible, choose a casual introductory reception instead of a formal luncheon or a theater-style company meeting.

HOW IMPORTANT IS STYLE?

This debate springs up from time to time, especially during discussions about women's leadership. Many female leaders think style is crucial. In fact, some believe it is more important than substance. Here's where I land on the debate: It isn't critical, and it's certainly not more important than authenticity and comfort. Ideally, celebrating life in your own skin will become your style. Otherwise, you're detailing the car before you've fixed the engine.

Barbara Corcoran, a grand dame of real estate in New York City, once discussed her early, financially strapped years and her determination to buy the most expensive clothing off the rack. She wanted to look like who she wanted to be—a major success. I'm sure she is right, since in real estate, a look of success is smart. However, I am also willing to bet that her level of comfort with herself and the image she presented were just as important. If what you need to play at the top of your game is a particular look or flair, then go for it. If designer clothes bolster your self-confidence—and you can afford the time and money they require—shop on. I am merely suggesting that a "look" isn't the only thing that works. For some, style means a gym workout or an art class. What makes Oprah so engaging? It's not what she wears—I think it's that she is so much fun and seems so comfortable with who she is, flaws and all. It's a magnetic kind of style.

YOUR STARTING APPROACH

Regardless of your position or industry, good leaders focus on how they can harness and expand the capacities of the organization. There are a number of ways to inspire others to believe in and follow you, which in turn allows you to help them achieve their greatest potential.

• **Be the bartender—encourage people to talk.** Listen carefully to what your key players say. Be sure they believe that you will be fair and that you understand their issues and dilemmas. Learn your team's challenges, goals, and individual aspirations. Find out their triggers, passions, and what keeps them awake at night.

• **Be honest and direct.** Don't make promises you can't keep, but do make an honest commitment to address concerns that have merit. And if you already know about limitations or restrictions, tell your people now. Let them know that organizational success depends on individual success.

• **Share your vision and your anchors.** Your anchors tide your employees over until you can develop your agenda.

• **Use your sense of humor.** Don't forget to have fun! Be optimistic and upbeat. Who would you rather work with—Sarah Jessica Parker or Leona Helmsley? You don't need to be a clown-college graduate; just keep your perspective and allow yourself to be entertained. Nobody wants to be the grim reaper's sidekick.

What Not to Do

- **Don't claim to have all the answers.** Let your people know that you will make decisions based on the best data available. Explain that you welcome their constructive advice.
- **Don't expect perfection in yourself or others.** People are loved for the combination of their skills and imperfections—the characteristics that make them human. The imperfections you beat yourself up about will make you approachable and accessible. You can't be a CFO with zero capacity for numbers, but you can be human without being incompetent or losing your credibility. Learn to laugh at yourself; it helps to blow off steam.

JUMPSTARTER: *DON'T UNDERESTIMATE THE IMPORTANCE OF THE FIRST TEAM MEETING*

I'm assuming you've had several prestart meetings with your boss. This means you have (1) a clear idea of the top tasks or outcomes expected of you, and (2) a plan for how the two of you will communicate. Now let's turn our attention to your direct reports.

Your First Team Meeting

In this first key meeting, it's important to engage in the following:

Get to Know Your Team. Connecting with your direct reports as a team should be one of your first priorities. Conduct your kick-off meeting in an open, comfortable setting with no tables. At the start of the meeting, introduce yourself. If you are new to the group, describe who you are, both professionally and personally, and how you came to be at the organization.

Whether you are hired from outside or promoted from within, your team will also want to know the following:

- Your approach to management and your leadership anchors
- Your hopes and aspirations for the next year
- What *success* means relative to how people work together and the climate of the larger organization
- What you think it's like to work with you—your quirks, habits, and concerns

Establish Behavioral Norms. Next, listen to your team members. What are their hopes for the working relationship? What are their concerns or fears? Discuss these issues as a team, and use that discussion to develop team norms—behaviors you agree to abide by when working together. Examples of team norms include procedural behaviors, such as agreeing to respond to e-mails within 24 hours or less, or behavioral norms, such as agreeing to settle disputes at the source rather than airing grievances in the parking lot. For some real-world examples of team norms, see Accelerator 4A in the Appendix.

Over time, you may want to return to your initial agreements and reevaluate them. Your fresh eyes may notice entrenched but counterproductive behaviors, such as using sarcasm to find fault indirectly, hesitation to challenge questionable ideas from superiors, or a tendency to focus on the "good old days" before the transition. Behavioral norms are the "facts on the ground" when you arrive, but that doesn't mean they're set in stone.

Communicate Your Entry Plan. Your third agenda item is to describe your entry plan: who you plan to spend time with, the challenges you've already identified, what you plan to learn, how your time will be spent, and your overall availability. Get team members' feedback on your plan, including who you should develop relationships with and any questions you should ask. Explain your plans for the transition team described in Chapter 6. Describe the transition team's role and boundaries, and ask for members' support (after all, their own direct reports will be taking time to participate).

If time allows in your first meeting, conduct a mini–strategy session. Articulate what you have already heard, then verify its accuracy. Finally, outline your general performance expectations. End the meeting by expressing your optimism, excitement, and appreciation for your team's hard work, both previously and in the future.

For a sample agenda outline to use in planning your first team meeting, see Accelerator 4B in the Appendix.

One-on-One Meetings with Your Direct Reports

Over the next few days, try to meet with each of your direct reports. Assure them that their jobs are safe if they can accomplish their goals. Give them a chance to avoid being labeled. Steer clear of interrogations, and acknowledge your dependence on them for institutional information and support.

LIN, ALLIE, AND ELAINE'S EXPECTATIONS IN THEIR FIRST TEAM MEETINGS

- **Lin** plans to integrate technical systems, improve internal service by 15 percent, and reduce the number of grievances by 50 percent.
- **Allie** plans to increase revenue by 20 percent in the first year and to identify and standardize the five most important services offered by her regional managers.
- **Elaine** plans to get her financially shaky hospital to break even within two years, make a 10 percent cut in department costs without reducing quality of service, and reduce turnover by improving staff morale.

Other Meetings

The rest of your initial meetings will be dictated by your entry plan, but you will certainly need to connect with other parties as well—whether it's the city council, the governing board, unions, the corporate office, important customers, major clients, shareholders, or other stakeholders. Get out there, talk to them, describe your anchors, and open the communication channels. If you have been promoted from within, you will know what strategic issues exist and can begin to address them quickly. If you're new to the organization, you will want to verify what you've learned.

COMBINE PROFESSIONAL AND PERSONAL CONNECTIONS

When you can connect personally, do so. When you can get on their turf, do that as well. Personal contact, especially on home ground, will limit the noise factor. Get on the plane, get out to the job sites, and visit constituents where they are. If it is not possible to make personal contact, consider other, creative ways to reach out, as these women leaders did:

ALLIE'S ONE-ON-ONE

Allie will carefully plan her approach to the man she bypassed for the job, then meet with him as quickly as possible. She will not mention the underlying friction, but she will be ready to respond if he brings it up ("I know it's awkward now, but I'm confident that we can get beyond this and do a great job together. The team needs you and your skills."). Allie will make sure he knows that she believes he is a skilled contributor and the team needs him, and that she looks forward to developing a good working relationship with him.

- "I personally interviewed my reports two levels down and held group meetings and focus groups with everyone else."
- "I wrote and distributed a description of my values and approach—what I want to model and reward."
- "I had a personal phone message created and sent it to everyone in the organization."
- "I wrote a letter to the entire hospital and community outlining what I considered top priorities and describing how we should interact with one another to achieve our mission."
- "I started a weekly newsletter, dedicating major sections to areas I knew we needed to improve both operationally and culturally."
- "I issued a set of 'core promises' to the staff and community."
- "I personally visited 70 units in our district to identify what was really happening out in the field."
- "I met with every department, explaining to them, 'This is what I value, these are the challenges I already know about, this is how my time will be spent, this is my availability, and this is my ideal leadership culture.'"

WHAT IT ALL MEANS

In the blur of activity that makes up the first 100 days on a job, the attention paid to communication is often inadequate—but first impressions about your character, values, and leadership style endure well into your tenure. In the pause between "take your mark" and "go," think about your first impression. Be sure that how, why, and when you manage your message is an integral part of your entry plan into your new position.

Your first actions will resonate like a timpani in a Quonset hut, so it pays to plan them well. Use Day One to establish an upbeat, can-do spirit with your team and get feedback on your entry plan. You're off to a strong start and are well prepared for the first 50 days.

☑ CHAPTER CHECKLIST

- ☐ I can identify potential activities to create a positive first impression.
- ☐ I know what symbolic gestures will support my desired first impression.
- ☐ I have explained to the appropriate people what they can do to help me create a positive first impression.
- ☐ Key players know my anchors, priorities, and work style.
- ☐ I understand the priorities of my key stakeholders.
- ☐ We are off to a strong start.

CHAPTER

The First 50 Days

BY NOW, YOU could be on the brink of data overload—processing strong impressions about the organization, operations, people, and performance. It's time to confirm or correct your working hypothesis, develop strategic alliances, manage your message, and look for quick successes. This chapter will guide you through the critical first few weeks. Ditch the jacket and roll up your sleeves, because we have lots of work to do.

THE BIG PICTURE

Seize the moment. Remember all those women on the *Titanic* who waved off the dessert cart.

—Erma Bombeck

The first few weeks are an opportunity. You can be "with" but not "of" the organization. During this period, you can have fresh eyes that allow you to see the organization or your new job from an objective perspective. Take advantage of your early tenure to really observe and understand what is going on.

For example, do you visit the sights in your own hometown? During my second year working in Kenya, my family came to visit. As we drove by markets, jacaranda trees, and the majestic Masai women, my sister yanked her camera out and snapped photos of everything, while I wondered, "What's so special about that scene?" She clicked and clicked while I groaned, "Not again." Her fresh eyes captured amazing visuals that had become ordinary to me.

Another advantage of these first few weeks is that you get to be new. You'll never again have the excuse of being naive and uninformed. Use that to your advantage. You can be artful with your questions, unearthing critical issues without making people defensive. People forgive your newness—for a while. Ask good questions now, and you're accessible. Ask the same questions later, and you're incompetent. The same burp that makes a baby adorable will get a five-year-old in big trouble. Remember to phrase your questions in ways that signal respectful inquiry rather than doubtful undermining.

It's a Demanding Time for Everyone

> You have a short window of time before you get "caught in the traffic" and can't see the road.
>
> —Medical rescue executive

You will feel the push to prove yourself quickly versus the pull to avoid bad mistakes. You know you need time for thorough analysis and thoughtful decisions, but you may feel simultaneous pressure to get something (anything!) accomplished immediately. You're pressed for time and must face complex circumstances with imperfect information. You're not alone. Unfortunately, women have few leadership opportunities to spare; a poorly executed beginning could blow your chance of success. In this case, it's worth measuring twice.

Leadership transitions are unsettling for everyone. Staff want to know where they stand, while your boss wants to know whether you're the right choice. People may be distracted or nervous about their futures and will try to squeeze meaning from any comment or gesture you make or any rumor they hear.

COMMON TRANSITION MISTAKES

My first overseas assignment was directing a rural health care facility in Kenya, where malaria took the lives of many infants. "How hard can it be?" I thought, as the airplane landed. "We'll just teach the local people about standing water, mosquitoes, and prophylaxes. We'll eradicate malaria in two years." My zest was surpassed only by my naiveté. I went in with no clue of the time, patience, and resources required to tackle such an enormous health problem.

Eager to make quick progress and establish credentials, new leaders sometimes make hasty personnel decisions or operational shake-ups. Proceed with extreme caution. If you cut staff immediately, you risk creating a blame culture, limiting trust, and losing critical institutional knowledge. Under most circumstances, it's best to avoid a company shake-up until you know more. No need to throw out either the baby or the bathwater just yet.

For example, Jenny was selected as vice president for a large financial services firm after a trusted consultant had declined the job because it would require a cross-country relocation. Before she began, he pulled her aside to say, "If you want credibility in this job, you are going to have to make a decisive move immediately. I know this company. Trust me, you need to get rid of the following top layers of management." He proceeded to tell her the people who should be axed. Despite the strong pressure, Jenny was convinced she needed to wait until she was in the position a while and could personally evaluate the situation. After a few weeks, she realized the people the consultant had targeted were those who had resisted his change efforts—and for good reason. He had made some potentially disastrous blunders. Jenny did eventually make a decisive move: She fired the consultant! Had she started work with her mind made up, she would have made a huge personal, professional, and strategic mistake.

Don't assume from your prework observations and readings that you know the people or organization. Start your first 50 days with a clean slate and fresh eyes. First impressions may last, but they aren't always accurate.

For example, I learned about the fallacy of first impressions when renting office space from an accounting firm whose receptionist was a 40-year-old divorced woman with four children and a high-school degree. The place would have imploded without her, but given her enormous personal responsibilities, I assumed she was an extremely hard worker who only had time for family and her job. Imagine my surprise and awe when I learned she had served on the founding board of Plenty, an organization that won the Right Livelihood (a highly prized international peace award).

The cost of failure is enormous in terms of time, money, and momentum. You are not the only one at risk when you take a new job. Therefore, consider yourself one of the team, with others sharing a stake in your success.

I always feel pity—and amazement—when I hear goalkeepers in soccer berate themselves for missing a block. From my soccer mom's lawn-chair perspective, the ball has to blast through nine other players to get to that final shot. Likewise, transitions are a group effort.

JUMPSTARTER: *LISTEN, LEARN, AND CONFIRM*

In your first 50 days, be ready to listen with an empathetic but discerning ear. Your job is to learn and confirm what you can by finalizing your transition plan, then following up and making every interaction count.

As a group, women tend to be problem solvers. As you listen over the next couple of weeks, remember to look beyond what needs to be fixed. Be sure to also identify what needs to be preserved and/or avoided.

Measures of Success

In the first few weeks, learn how success is measured for each of your major responsibilities and how those areas are doing relative to the specified measurements. Is individual performance linked to organizational performance? If not, that should become one of your first year's priorities.

When meeting with your major constituents (boss, staff, teammates, internal or external customers, shareholders, and so on), learn their perceptions of operational strengths, weaknesses, and success.

History and Its Impact on Current and Future Practices

Your entry plan includes understanding how corporate history has influenced current operations. Once you begin work, you can dig much deeper into the rich store of available information. Talk to the old-timers. Learn the corporate stories and anecdotes; they make up the culture, and the culture is the foundation of the organization. You cannot plan to make sweeping changes before understanding the roots of the current belief system.

For example, in a well-funded municipal department, a new leader was astounded that divisions refused to share resources, information, or good ideas. Digging deeper, the manager learned that in leaner financial years—when staff did agree to loan tools and major equipment to other sections—they were slapped with harsh reprimands and budget adjustments. "If they have more than they need, they don't need more," was the reasoning. "You loan, you lose" became a de facto slogan. Although the department had gotten out of its financial rut, the possessive attitude remained.

THE PEOPLE

> Don't let the "meet and greet" get in the way of your analysis. Instead, make it part of your analysis.
>
> —Medical executive

Learn who will be important to your success. Your plan should include how you'll get to know them. It will typically include the individuals outlined here.

Your Boss

By now, you should know the boss's take on the organization's strategic direction and, specifically, what is expected of you. Learn how he or she wants to communicate and be kept informed. Here are some other thoughts for managing your boss:

- Part of your job is to make your boss's job easier. Examine issues from his or her point of view.
- If you are presenting a problem, always offer a potential solution.
- Be sure you have the authority you need to get the job done.
- If you expect resistance to female leadership, ensure that your boss doesn't allow an end run around your authority. Make sure he or she gives you the chance to handle an employee problem first.
- Never whine or complain, even when your fellow team members are slow to accept you as a colleague.

The Senior Team

You met with your direct reports on Day One. Over the next few days, meet with them individually in order to learn the following:

- Their goals and how they are doing relative to those goals
- How performance is measured in each area and how close individuals are to their goals
- Priorities, key relationships, and boundaries of authority
- What they consider to be your role and what support they need from you
- How they think decisions are really made
- What suggestions they have for you to accelerate your learning
- Their suggestions for an early win

When setting expectations for staff, emphasize that implementing change will be part of their job duties.

Assume there will be some "hazing." Boys learn from an early age to challenge the hierarchy. It's just a more sophisticated form of rutting. It's unpleasant and stressful, but if you're strong, direct and clear, you'll come through it successfully.

The Customers and Clients

Set the tone with your clients by using your newness to learn how they feel. Learn what they think about the current level of service (what does and doesn't work) and their priorities for working with you. If you are being hired to make changes, consider talking to disenfranchised customers and stakeholders too. They may have a valuable and unique perspective, and they'll likely be grateful for the attention.

Unions

> Our unions knew more about our new city manager's background than the city council did!
>
> —City contract manager

If you are in a union environment, you will want to learn how effective the unions are, how they use their power, and their take on the history of the working relationship with management. Don't be surprised if they know a lot about you!

JUMPSTARTER: *LEVERAGE YOUR RELATIONSHIPS*

> Women enter the job arena with a stronger urge to form and maintain relationships than men do.
>
> —Gail Evans, *Play Like a Man, Win Like a Woman*

By now you know what other relationships you need to develop: major clients, corporate players, constituents, and informal leaders. As I keep repeating: Get out and talk to them. Find out their issues, concerns, hopes, and priorities. Go out of your way to make everyone feel included. Avoid calling people into your office, which may set up an unintended power dynamic. Instead, go where they are comfortable and can speak freely. Look for work-related problems you can tackle together. Take advantage of your natural tendencies to make others feel comfortable and promote trust to create strong relationships. It will come in handy later on.

Determine what each of your contacts may want to learn from you and what you can do to develop credibility and trust. Use the chart provided in Accelerator 5A in the Appendix as a guide.

Your boss (or board) doesn't want any surprises but does want reassurance that you are the right person for the job. Plan to keep him or her informed of what you are learning and what conclusions you are developing. Emphasize what's working. Remember to check in with the boss regularly and to promote your successes.

Your executive team and direct reports want to know where they stand and what will be expected of them. They want to know if you are someone they can trust and respect. Acknowledge their contributions to date. Tell them what you expect and when you will establish performance standards. Assure them that you will keep the same team, providing that challenges are met. If it's true, emphasize that the job is theirs to lose. For example, when Ellen took over her CEO position, she told her staff that she assumed everyone was doing A+ work. She then explained that, based on her conversations with the board, changes were coming. As long as the executives could adapt to the changes, their jobs were secure.

Staff members want to know what will be changing and what will be remaining the same, assurance that you have their best interests in mind, freedom to do their job in the best way they know, acknowledgment for their contributions, and whether you are credible and trustworthy. As much as possible, reassure them by describing your anchors, announcing current priorities and initiatives, and providing a time line for further information and direction.

Clients, constituents, and customers want to know whether you have their interests in mind and are prepared to listen and respond to their issues. Explain how you will keep them informed and what they can expect.

If You Are Leading Others Who Were Finalists for Your Job

First, be thankful. You have probably inherited talented staff. Treat them no differently than your other staff. Let them know you rely on their expertise. If you meet resistance, avoid jumping to conclusions based on funky dynamics. Separate fact from interpretation.

For example, Harriett is the CEO of a well-funded agency. Her direct report, an attorney, loved catching her in a mistake or otherwise off guard. Initially Harriett was annoyed by his self-satisfied smirks, but she eventually realized that his fine, skeptical mind was an asset in her decision-making process. She learned to preempt his combativeness by saying, "Tell me how this can go wrong." Overnight, she both legitimized the challenges and gained a fiercely loyal staff member.

A male colleague who has recently been snubbed may either close up or come out snarling. He may try hard to make your life miserable since women typically back down from conflict. However, if you are clear, stick to your purpose, and openly engage your team, even the most recalcitrant members will eventually go along. Once he knows you're in charge and mean business, he'll probably become a strong team player.

JUMPSTARTER: *MANAGE YOUR MESSAGE*

Articulating your anchors will be part of your initial message in the first 50 days. The rest of your communication will be determined by the situation. You may not know your long-term agenda, but you will quickly learn the prevailing attitude of the staff.

Once you understand the situation from their point of view, craft your message accordingly. For instance, if there is low morale and little trust, you can manage your message by opening up meetings, encouraging questions, and emphasizing transparency in decision making. Alternatively, suppose you take over the chaos of a rapidly growing firm. Your first message may be to reassure staff, convey your plan and time lines, explain that discussions of priorities are forthcoming, and provide guarantees of what is not going to change.

Remember: no blame. Even if you are replacing Captain Ahab or Elmer Fudd, avoid criticizing your predecessor. Finding fault will only promote a counterproductive culture of blame. Encourage staff by emphasizing that your job is to make a good thing better by asking what they need, establishing yourself as a resource, calming apprehensions, and communicating through both word and deed that you are a team player.

See Accelerator 5B in the Appendix for more help in managing your message.

How Communication Goes Wrong

Communicating is easy; communicating effectively is not. Despite our technological advancements—and often because of them—the goal of reaching your audience with the message you intend is a challenge. Although you decide what you are trying to convey, your audience gets to decide what it means. More often than we realize, our messages spiral into an Abbott and Costello–style "Who's on first?" routine.

Organizational Context. If you are hired from outside—even from another department—you are entering a new culture with its own history, language, values, and practices. Sometimes innocent comments or actions are a blaring reminder that you're new and uninitiated. Small actions can produce big misunderstandings and harsh, knee-jerk reactions.

For example, a professional colleague (a civilian) meticulously researched and developed a training video for the armed services. Many hours and dollars later, the film was previewed and panned. Two military uniform ribbons in one tiny scene were inadvertently reversed—an error that compromised the credibility of the entire film. Good editing could save the film, but the filmmaker's credibility was lost.

There are subtle but similar cultural land mines in every organization. "Village" traditions can contribute to unintended message distortion that rivals the most contorted Escher engraving. Unwritten policies at one organization may be heretical at another. Watch closely to see what rules apply.

For example, your open-door policy at your last job may have been a wonderful management tool for promoting healthy communication. In your new leadership position, however, it could be considered a deliberate ploy to encourage employees to sidestep the current lines of authority. Different rules may apply.

Information Overload. We are constantly bombarded by information. David Adams noted in his article "Non-Verbal Communication: A Leader's Most Powerful, Revealing Tool" that the typical leader receives the following in an average day at the office:

- 46 phone calls
- 25 e-mails (When's the last time you received only 25?)
- 23 postal items
- 16 voice mails
- 16 face-to-face contacts
- 9 mobile phone calls
- 8 interoffice memos

Whew! It's tiring just to *read* all that. This daily assault creates a worker with the attention span of a neurotic gnat. Given all this data smog, it is truly a wonder that we even know what day it is.

The trend will continue. One look at today's teenagers illustrates the multitasking future of communication. They write instant messages, listen to music, do their homework, and play computer games while talking on the phone. And many of them still make the honor roll.

The Need for Noise. With the accelerating barrage of data, our culture is becoming increasingly uncomfortable with silence. We have a tendency to "fill up the space" with activity or internal noise. Employees and colleagues are distracted and want to know what's coming. Lacking solid information, they will use any available data to fill in the blanks. Rumors travel like hurricanes through an organization. Misinformation and rumor can feel safer than no information at all.

Information Distortion: Lost in Space. Corporate communications must travel through incredible obstacles, bending and flexing until they may no longer resemble what the sender intended. Often, the problem occurs at the source with a poorly created message.

For example, Susan, the new boss, said she wanted a report to be "professional." She meant that she wanted accurate data. But in her company's traditional language, *professional* meant "slick graphics." When the sizable bill for the expensively produced report came in, Susan hit the roof. When someone fails to meet your expectations, learn what part you played in the problem.

Next, communication must overcome the most difficult obstacle of all: the internal noise of the receiver. Individual needs, values, attitudes, and beliefs are tightly woven filters through which messages must somehow pass. Since, according to Robert Bacal in his article "Improving Communication: Tips for Managers" (work911.com), the average leader spends up to 80 percent of her time communicating, the potential for misunderstanding is enormous. This is particularly difficult if you find yourself in an organization where trust is low.

A Women's Guide to Communication

As women leaders find their way in a classically male-dominated environment, they must adopt behaviors (assertiveness, for example) that contradict our historic interpretation of the way females are. If women in a particular work environment have traditionally been soft-spoken support staff, a message from a forceful female leader might be met with resistance. As above, so below—women who stereotypically conform to traditional support roles are considered poor leadership choices, yet those who pursue leadership positions may be considered failures as wives and mothers or too masculine for their own good.

Sometimes and in some industries, women are allowed a smaller arsenal of acceptable management practices. If too directive, they risk being labeled a bitch. Of course, the label is just name-calling unless it causes staff to resist your leadership. Calling a strong female leader a bitch laughably automatic response by the insecure, but it still finds a lot of traction in our culture. However, too much emphasis on the softer style of building rapport will probably result in a challenge to a female leader's authority. As Deborah Tannen states in her book, *Talking from 9 to 5*, "Wearing the mantle of authority lightly allows it to be more easily pushed off your shoulders."

Politically Correct Caution Can Reduce Authenticity. The growth in female leadership has contributed to cautious communication. It is so darn easy to offend, insult, or violate that banter and spontaneity sometimes give way to more carefully studied and oddly stilted conversation. This includes conflict. Since males grow up "duking" it out, they are more comfortable and even enjoy a good argument. Most females would rather get their teeth drilled. Though few would argue against the value of diversity, sometimes the resulting hypersensitivity affects everyone's ability to be genuine.

Women Tend to Self-Limit. Women often limit themselves during communication for two primary reasons. The first is simple habit. Some communication patterns we established growing up are instinctive but no longer useful. Didn't your mom tell you that it's not nice to argue? Well, perhaps that doesn't apply when negotiating multimillion-dollar deals.

Second, ineffective communication can reflect a lack of personal confidence. Women who doubt themselves may reflexively look to others for support and agreement. Not only is organizational leadership new, intimidating arena, but women are more relationship-oriented than men. Their sense of self-worth comes, in part, from the collective support of others. Therefore, instead of moving a meeting forward by saying, "Let's continue," such women might ask, "Is it OK to move on?"

Ms. Communication: How Women Make "Message Mistakes"

There are enough leadership pitfalls without digging your own. Yet, sometimes women make minor communication mistakes that result in long-term disaster. Informed feedback, awareness, and practice can help you avoid the following tendencies.

Overusing Tentative Language or Tone. Consider the sentence "Perhaps we should think about increasing the advertising budget." The speaker really wants to expand marketing, but her indefinitely worded suggestion allows room for others to disagree. She thinks she is being a team player. However, overuse of this language may cause her staff to wonder if she has what it takes to survive heated negotiations. A better approach would be "For desired results, we'll need to increase the advertising budget."

A typical faux pas is to elevate vocal inflection at the end of a sentence, which makes the statement resemble a question—that is, "I am assuming we want to proceed with this project?" This is a typically female habit that reveals a reluctance to give an opinion directly. A better approach would be "Let's proceed with this project." Or, if you do want to ask a question, go ahead and really ask it: "Do you want to proceed with this project?"

Overusing Questions. Observe any social setting and you'll see that women ask more questions than men, often **to develop rapport**.

Men, however, typically ask questions to get information; establishing a relationship is less important. In fact, men are more driven to develop a social hierarchy than to establish a common connection. The female tries for egalitarianism, while the male jostles to establish pecking order.

Just as in a social situation, overuse of questions in a professional context can be interpreted (consciously or unconsciously) in a negative way. "Wow, she sure asks a lot of questions," thinks your listener. "I must know more than she does, which means I have the advantage."

A better approach would be to keep mental track of the questions you ask and your motive for asking them. Note how often your new colleagues ask questions versus your own running total.

Women sometimes use questions **to divert attention away from themselves.** Be careful; don't let questions play such a central role in your communications that you lose your own voice and gradually become ignored. A better approach would be to balance your need to know with a need to inform.

Women often engage by asking questions and drawing others out. Asking "Can you get this done in three months?" seems considerate rather than demanding. However, sometimes you need to direct. That's why you are in charge. In those cases, state your directive clearly: "The deadline for this project is three months. Tell me what you need to get it done."

Giving In and Being Polite. In conflict, women are more likely than men to give in when they perceive the relationship (personal or professional) is at stake. If they must choose between winning the argument and maintaining the relationship, women often choose the latter. The personal conflict is too stressful.

Thanks to Title IX—legislation that requires all schools receiving federal funds to provide girls an equal opportunity to compete in sports—this is changing. As girls receive more opportunities in the rough-and-tumble world of team sports, they are improving their sparring techniques. Like their male counterparts, they can duke it out in competition, then throw their arms around their adversary's shoulders once the contest is over. However, for many, comfort with competition continues to be a problem.

Remember that leadership is controversial. You can expect some people to dislike you, your message, or your anchors, despite your best efforts. Practice mentally separating your need for connection from the situation in front of you. Keep in mind that it's the issue at risk, not the relationship.

Women often allow their male colleagues to interrupt. They may think they are being polite, when in fact they are giving ground to a power play. Hold your hand up (palm out) to the interrupter and say, "I'd like to complete my thought." When you finish, yield the floor on your own terms.

Failing to Take Credit for Accomplishments. It is important to share credit, but too often women give it all away. They somehow think that the work speaks for itself. It won't. People listen to other people, not to the work.

Keep your boss and other key players informed of your successes by mentioning them in meetings, newsletters, or the corridor. Fire off an e-mail or memo. Be the first to announce good news and you'll be associated with it. You can even encourage others you trust to promote your successes. You'd do the same for them, wouldn't you?

Apologizing Too Quickly. Save the apologies for your own errors. If someone complains about a tough situation, a sympathetic "I'm sorry" implies you're somehow to blame. New women leaders also find themselves automatically apologizing, as in, "I'm sorry, but I just started. Can you explain that again?" Using *sorry* as a verbal crutch or way to relate is weak and meaningless.

A better approach would be "Sounds like it was difficult for you to get your point across," or "I'd like to understand how this policy was developed. Can you explain it to me?"

Criticizing Indirectly. Hoping to soften the blow, women sometimes criticize indirectly. How often have you heard a superficial compliment immediately followed by a criticism? As when someone begins, "That's a good idea, but . . . ." My father used to say, "It's the *buts* that get you every time" because the speaker's punch line—and real message—follows that three-letter word.

Be clear and direct about what you do and don't like. Peppering criticism with flattery diminishes the effectiveness of both. For example, try, "I think your report is quite good. The language is clear and the purpose well-stated. Adding examples and expanding the summary will improve it."

Relying on Verbal Crutches. Women cannot afford lazy communication habits. Filler words such as *um* and *ah* tell your audience that you're unsure of yourself or unprepared. Repeating throat-clearing introductory words such as *basically* or *essentially* also grates on your audience.

Ask trusted colleagues or family whether or not you have this habit. If necessary, replace the filler words with pauses. People probably won't notice your silences, but they will start mentally counting your *kindas*, *as a matter of facts*, or *likes*!

Shifting to Past Tense. Women unconsciously shift to the past tense when they become unsure of their opinions or when their convictions begin to waver. "I was thinking that the budget figure is too high," says the executive who expects immediate contradiction. This is often the first indicator that she is beginning to back down from her position. Keeping your language active and in the present tense maintains audience engagement and makes you appear confident in your convictions.

LIN'S COMMUNICATION CHALLENGES

Lin asks close colleagues about her communication style and learns two interesting facts. First, when Lin disagrees with someone's comment, she pauses and sets her jaw. Second, they know she is unsure of herself when she switches to the past tense. When that happens, her message loses its punch. She's glad to know about these tendencies because she is inheriting some surly technical staff who will challenge her often. She cannot afford to seem uncertain.

A better approach would be "My first reaction is that the budget figure is too high. However, I would like to have more discussion on this."

The Three Components of Great Communication

The foundation of great communication requires paying attention to you, your message, and your audience. The chart in Accelerator 5C in the Appendix can help you plan for all three.

You. Be who you are, flaws and all. As mentioned previously, you need to be comfortable in your own skin. Accept who you are and try to limit or purge the self-doubt and mental noise. Your confidence motivates others to learn more about you, limiting misunderstanding on their end. Accept your weaknesses as part of the package. As long as they are not fatal career flaws, shortcomings make you more human and approachable. Actresses like Meg Ryan and Sandra Bullock capitalize on their down-to-earth personas as much as their appearance and talent. When describing a very successful but intimidating political leader, my friend Sharon said, "I knew I liked her when I heard she locked her keys in her car four times in one week." Remember, you don't need to be one of the boys. You just need to understand them. Your value comes from your diversity.

Have the courage to live your values. Your unconscious actions and reactions reflect your deeply held beliefs. Your credibility will be determined, in part, by the consistency between what you say and how you behave. Be ready to live your values at work now, even though it's sometimes tough. Communicating and living by your anchors will support your efforts to stay strong.

For example, while interviewing for an executive position, Eileen visited the office just as her potential boss was yelling at a subordinate. Confronting her boss-to-be, Eileen emphasized that she would not work in an environment that condoned behavior so contrary to her values of mutual respect. She made her point, he made a change, and she has been successful in promoting a much healthier work atmosphere.

Be predictable, purposeful, and confident. Staff are trying to figure you out, not to mention your personal style and plans. It's a vulnerable time in the organization, and behaving erratically will only increase anxiety. People need assurance that you are consistent, predictable, and strong. They want to be led.

Get feedback. You only have to see one Robert De Niro movie to notice how much communication goes on at the unspoken (or unconscious) level. Ask others you trust how you either promote or discourage effective communication.

Broaden your communication style. Research done by Pat Vaughn Tremmel, published in "Women Most Effective Leaders for Today's World" (American Association for the Advancement of Science), shows that the communication style typically used by women will be more effective with today's generation of workers. However, just as some dominant men can benefit from including others in their decision making, many women could sometimes toughen up and get more assertive and directive.

If you struggle with speaking out and expressing your ideas—especially contentious ideas—there's a good historical reason. In *Eloquence in an Electronic Age: The Transformation of Political Speechmaking*, Kathleen Hall Jamieson says,

> Throughout history, silence was the price a woman paid to stay safe. In seventeenth-century America, an "unquiet" woman was punished on the dunking stool. With each plunge, the breathless "harpy" was commanded to renounce her verbal past. In Massachusetts, more "witches" were convicted of "assaultive speech" than any other crime.

Silence may be ladylike, but it is not necessarily leaderlike. Step out of those learned behaviors and speak your piece. Or as a United Way director and former Procter & Gamble executive put it,

> Women need to be better at "loose-tight" communication. Loose is the softer, nurturing side, while tight is the more authoritative, "if you don't do it, I'm going to kick your ass" response. One time, I accompanied my HR executive boss to lunch with a candidate for a high-level sales position. She asked the candidate's expectations about compensation, and he threw out a large number. Her response was, "You're out of your **** mind." She had loose and tight down pat.

Build trust and credibility. In any dialogue, there are three simultaneous conversations: the discussion itself and each person's internal commentary. If you lack credibility, the mental banter trumps the spoken word. For instance, you make an innocent comment about a production schedule to someone who has little confidence in your abilities. In that person's mind, the mental Q&A does you no favors: "Why does she want to mess with my schedule? She doesn't have any expertise here. I better go back and warn the folks on the floor. How do I keep her out of my business?" And so on. Building trust and credibility with those around you limits this kind of static. The more they like you, the more they'll trust your intentions.

Who you are can be louder than what you say. Just as important as what you actually say is the congruence between what you say and what you ultimately do—or don't do. What seems rather simple on the surface can present some difficult choices.

For example, Claire encouraged transparency in communication and zealously created a website dedicated to open lines of communication with everyone in the organization. Then an anonymously posted question took a deliberate potshot at her decisions and authority. If she shuts down the website in response, the obvious message is that she can't handle criticism, and from then on, such condemnation will stay behind her back and underground, where she can't confront it. If she truly believes in transparency, she'll post a response that thanks the creator of the message and answers it in the most diplomatic, mature, productive way she can manage.

The Message. Your message goes beyond words; words are just a part of the message. Research conducted by Albert Mehrabian, professor emeritus of psychology at the University of California in Los Angeles, concluded that what you actually say provides less than 10 percent of the data people instinctively use to react positively or negatively. Mehrabian found that audiences are far more likely to respond unconsciously to your voice and facial expressions, especially if they send messages inconsistent with what you're actually saying. Pay attention to the nonverbal cues you deliver, using people you trust as informed sounding boards. Are you telling people to calm down while nervously jingling your keys? Though that's preferable to some parallel behaviors in men—at least women jingling their keys don't appear to be rearranging their genitalia, nervously or otherwise. Your words can be upbeat and optimistic, but what is your body language saying? Slumped shoulders can negate an hour of executive cheer-leading. Even if it requires an Oscar-worthy performance, you will need to "fake it till you make it," or as Peggy Klaus, author of *Brag: The Art of Tooting Your Own Horn Without Blowing It*, says, "Act as if."

What about your facial cues? John Gottman of the University of Washington conducted some fascinating studies of newly-wed expressions. Over 40 sets of muscles in the face allow us to express emotion or interest. We are often unaware of how much "skepticism, disgust, anxiety or boredom we are revealing in our faces." He discovered that nonverbal communications among married couples, such as rolling eyes or curling lips, played a key role in predicting who would be divorced three years later. If you aren't aware of what your nonverbal messages are, ask people you trust to tell you about them.

Keep it positive. Find and emphasize what's going well, no matter how difficult the situation. There's a reason you chose the job. Whether it's your belief in the mission, the organization's reputation, or the employees' expertise, talk about what you've seen that you admire and want to maintain. Be careful, though: Insincere flattery is a surefire way to lose credibility.

For example, Louis replaced a popular leader at a West Coast leadership school. He observed a course delivered by leadership trainers and wrote a formal letter of commendation to the entire training staff as a follow-up. Unfortunately, a third of the recipients of the letter were on vacation during the class and had not even met their new boss. Naturally, they questioned his motives for writing the letter, labeling it empty flattery instead of genuine praise.

Keep your message simple, strong, constant, and consistent. You can minimize the chance for distortion by being simple, clear, and strong with your message. In the words of one turn-around executive, who has pulled four high-profile nonprofit organizations from spiraling death spins, "I say over and over that I am here for one reason only, to fulfill our mission. Before long, I can hear them repeat the mission back to me word for word."

Which of the following messages would you remember?

- Our operations will be excellent. We will work hard to continually minimize the need to reinspect or rework assembled products.
- We get it right the first time, every time.

Speaking of which, avoid the female tendency to get the words "absolutely" right, which may result in overexplanations and longer phrasing. Be brief and powerful with your language.

Limit your communication to no more than five major points, expressed clearly and with power. For instance, here's the message of an admiral who leads thousands: "One, innovate; two, enable innovation; and three, past practices are relevant, but don't let them bog us down."

Communicate often. You will have to compete with other information. Make communication ongoing. Do not underestimate the number of times and ways you will need to deliver your message so that the entire organization understands it.

When developing communication plans for reaching out, consider the 3 × 3 approach: Convey each important message three times in three different ways. For instance, if you want to signal that management is accessible, institute informal receptions or brown-bag lunches; issue a newsletter welcoming comments; and allow anonymous questions in large staff meetings.

Seize each moment. Be clear enough on your message or learning objectives that you can make every interaction count. Remember that your first 100 days are your only chance to make a great first impression.

Use anecdotes, stories, metaphors, and symbols. The power of your message increases dramatically when you punch it up with illustrations that your audience can relate to—especially those anecdotes collected during your due diligence.

For example, Felicity wanted to emphasize to her sales force the importance of friendly service that goes the extra mile. So she told a story about how one salesman had dropped off a customer's lost wallet on his way home from work. He had quite literally gone the extra mile.

Remember to include symbolic actions as well. One CFO of a successful health care facility says the first thing she does is "paint the lobby"—that is, institute some physical improvement. She wants to send the message that she is ready and willing to make positive changes. Another turnaround executive always fixes up the workplace first, a signal to employees that they are her most important customers.

Don't underestimate the power of symbolic gestures. Wear work boots to the job site, replace the square conference table with a round one, park in the employee lot, and don't hide behind podiums and lecterns.

Know how much information is enough. Even if your organization is wired for good communication, it's tough to determine the appropriate level of information. Given too much, employees will respond by deleting e-mails unread or tuning out in meetings. Too little, and you risk alienation. Half-shaped or evolving messages can lead to confusion and frustration.

One organization suffered lost time and resentment when employees acted on general ideas bounced around by their senior manager. The manager thought he was brainstorming. The employees thought he was giving orders.

Consider asking your staff how much information they need. Do they want to hear ideas that are not final or fully formed? One option is to reach out with your short, powerful messages, then make the secondary information available via other media (such as newsletters or websites). Let others know where additional information is available (as in meeting minutes).

The Audience. It's not what you say, it's what they "get." In *Strategic Communication Management* magazine, Ed Robertson discusses the myth that *communication* and *information* are synonymous. He counters by explaining that "information is not made meaningful to another person until it is processed." People are looking for data, and they have a way of filling in the information gaps with "noise"—often inaccurately. Remember, you get to decide what to say, but your audience gets to decide what it means. Your goal is to ensure that the message you send is the message they truly receive.

For example, Robin works in a car wash on a sunny day. Business is brisk, and she has been working nonstop for six hours straight—no break, no lunch. Exhausted, she plops down on the wall outside to catch her breath. Some waiting customer shoots her a glare. Robin is a great worker. She was overdue for a break. However, guess who just decided that the service at this car wash is terrible and is going to go tell all her friends? What message did Robin unintentionally deliver? Lousy service. Not fair, not accurate, but that's the "unmanaged" message nevertheless.

Look for ways to understand and manage your audience's decoding process. That car wash needs an employee lounge. You, on the other hand, may need a transition team. Detailed in Chapter 6, the transition team is a group of trusted employees and colleagues who can help you manage your communication by providing a means to test your message, help you learn the culture, and give you critical feedback.

Learn what's important to your audience. As Carol Gallagher wrote in *Going to the Top: A Road Map for Success from America's Leading Women Executives*, "For great ideas to turn into great solutions, they have to fall on ears that are ready to hear them." You must understand the needs and values of your audience if you want to reach them with your message. Learn what is important to them. Is it job security? Fulfilling work? Clear direction? If you discuss customer service when they are anxious about workforce reductions, you might as well be speaking Swahili in Chongqing.

Test your message. Your transition team (see Chapter 6) is a cross-representative group you can rely on throughout your 100-day start-up. Chosen well, they will offer priceless advice on how to navigate the organization. Use your transition team to explain how things really get done and to provide feedback on your plans. As you develop rapport and observe individuals prior to and early in your tenure, you can select candidates for the group. This guiding coalition will serve as a vital communication link.

Learn what captures your audience's attention. To communicate effectively with an audience, figure out what captures their attention. This requires experience synthesizing all of the aspects of your message into a coherent whole, as well as observing audience reactions.

Though it's a generalization, men tend to use humor to stir things up or challenge, while women use it to reduce tension, disarm, or equalize. When a series of bank robberies occurred in a Western state, a disgusted police chief sniped at his harried detectives, "I just tried to withdraw cash from my bank, but they're out of money." It was a deliberate attempt to goad them. Compare that to humor designed to ease the tension: "OK, detectives, we need to get a move on catching these guys. Let's question everyone we see in Armani or Gucci."

JUMPSTARTER: *IDENTIFY QUICK SUCCESSES*

Women need quick wins to solidify their credibility. Their leadership position is often tenuous until they can prove themselves. In your first 50 days, look for short-term wins that will create forward momentum and shore up your position. Short-term successes are the "low-hanging fruit," the easy projects or initiatives that have a good chance of success and high visibility.

ALLIE'S COMMUNICATION PLAN

Who You Are

What are the anchors you will convey in your first communications?	1. Let's do what it takes to get the job done. 2. Be who you are, be what you will, but be honest.
What do you know about your communication style and patterns?	I'm straightforward and direct, and I have no patience for idle chitchat. This will help as I set expectations, but I need people to be willing to come to me with issues.
What do you need to keep in mind as you craft your message?	Others want to get to know me. We can do this.

Your Message

Objectives: What do you want to accomplish (e.g., promote action, a feeling, awareness, commitment)?	1. Promote trust (despite my youth) in my leadership. 2. Create willingness for stores to try new activities and projects. 3. Raise awareness that things are going to "tighten up."
What message do you need to convey?	1. We need mutual honesty and respect. 2. We will combine efficiency with creativity.
Methods/Channels: What are the most effective methods	1. Conduct personal meetings with next two levels down.

and channels for delivering your messages to different audiences (e.g., written, oral, e-mail, paper, in person)?	2. Road show! I need to visit multiple sites. 3. Create clear workbooks to describe policy changes.
How is the organization set up for communication? Are those avenues appropriate for your message?	1. We have biweekly meetings. 2. Meetings are good forums, but infrequent. I will need to supplement them with additional communication channels.
Symbols: Are there other, more creative ways to deliver the message? If so, what are they?	Periodic reports on progress Items in the newsletter

Your Audience(s)

Who needs to receive the message?	1. Stores 2. Regional managers 3. My boss and his boss
What does your audience care about?	Store staff—Make our lives easier. Regional managers—Don't let us get caught in the middle. Tie us into the results. Give us job security. Boss—Improve the bottom line.
How can you tie your message to what is important to your audience?	If they do what I am recommending, we can increase profits while streamlining systems. Everyone wins.

For example, a midsize city council created a "City Vision"—a large-scale change effort designed to mobilize the community to create major upgrades. Many of the initiatives (better transportation, encouragement of tourism, anti-gang initiatives, and so on) were controversial and required widespread community involvement. The first effort was to paint the town's local eyesore: a water tower. Savvy leaders then used the edifice as a symbol for their efforts. It was an easy fix that helped create momentum for other, more complex initiatives.

Consider initiatives with the following qualities:

- Have a high probability of success and visibility
- Are relatively noncontroversial within the organization
- Might showcase or employ your unique strengths
- Emerge from your research.

Ask your stakeholders about what short-term initiative would mobilize and inspire the organization. For example, Helen, the city manager, knows she is a gifted dealmaker. She negotiated a tricky municipal land-use initiative as her first visible action. She

LIN'S EARLY WIN

Lin must improve administrative internal service, but long-standing turf wars and a culture of blame have limited useful problem solving and conversation. Since Lin lacks the political "baggage" of the other long-term employees, she feels certain she can lead a joint session that will air the issues and generate agreed-upon standards. If successful, the other senior staff will get the service they need, and the administrative division will get the respect they deserve.

also delayed tough personnel issues until the staff and city council, ecstatic after the land victory, rallied around her.

To evaluate possible ideas for quick successes, use the matrix in Accelerator 5D in the Appendix.

ELAINE'S EARLY WINS

With her hospital in desperate financial trouble and morale at rock bottom, Elaine must choose her first activities carefully. If her early efforts are successful, she believes she can convince the community to pass a parcel tax on the next ballot. The public's faith in her leadership will be critical to the future of the hospital.

Knowing she must quickly demonstrate savings without reducing service or affecting patient outcomes, Elaine determines the following potential early wins:

- Get additional help for nonmedical activities that take up too much nursing time, and limit the possible bed count (cuts time spent transporting charts, paperwork, and people; waiting for results or tests, and so forth).
- Contract out food services. Elaine knows that she can reduce the current $18 per lousy meal to $10 for a decent one.
- Negotiate a reciprocal deal with providers of redundant, costly services (such as CAT scans) and then cut the program out of the hospital.
- Install a pneumatic tube delivery system between the emergency department, lab, and other departments. This would be a relatively inexpensive investment and would reduce some annoying workload for the nurses.

(continued)

Elaine's Early Wins

Potential First Success	Likelihood of Success Within 100-Day Time Line	Visibility (internal and external)	Level of Support from Key Players (including transition team)	Investment Required
Additional nonprofessional help	Excellent	Good	Excellent	Minimal; will tap volunteer system first
Contract food services	Good	Good	Mixed; staff loyalty exists	Medium
Cut redundant diagnostic tool	Unknown	High; could be a political powder keg	Mixed	Minimal
Install pneumatic delivery system	Good	Good	Excellent	Medium

The Sweet Spot

Occasionally, your transition is the catalyst for a much-needed change. Constituents may be locked in old controversies or dilemmas but ready for a shift. An initiative is waiting for the right person to come along. With a little luck, you can find that sweet spot, a place where just the right action can yield immediate and visible rewards.

WHAT IT ALL MEANS

The first phase of your new position will focus on confirming your hypothesis, connecting with key players, managing your message, and snooping around for short-term victories. It's overwhelming, exciting, exhausting, and exhilarating. Remember to keep your sense of humor, have fun, and take care of yourself. Even if you live to work, working yourself to death won't impress anyone but the undertaker. And there are more than enough steps remaining in a successful transition to satisfy the most dedicated workaholic. You're only just beginning.

ALLIE HUNTS FOR THE SWEET SPOT

Allie knows a sweet spot that's a potential early win. As a teenager, she worked in the truck-stop convenience stores she now manages. She knows all the ways employees pilfer from the business, including charging (but not ringing up) locker room showers, cash-checking fees, and other cash services. She quickly runs the numbers and figures she can save the company more than $1 million by installing some very simple accounting safeguards.

☑ CHAPTER CHECKLIST

- ☐ I have confirmed and corrected my working hypothesis.
- ☐ I have connected with all the key players and know their concerns and priorities.
- ☐ The organization understands my personal priorities (my anchors).
- ☐ I understand what the organization needs from me.
- ☐ I have carefully planned my communication.
- ☐ My support systems are in place.
- ☐ I know the message I want to communicate; it is simple, clear, and powerful.
- ☐ I understand the organization's cultural nuances (baggage) that may affect my communication.
- ☐ I have translated my anchors into the language of the organization.
- ☐ I know my own communication strengths and limitations.
- ☐ I have identified several possible "first wins."

CHAPTER

Transition Teams

THE FIRST 100 days comprise a vulnerable time. The pressure of absorbing data, negotiating tricky relationships, and learning a new job or culture is daunting. A transition team can be an excellent support mechanism for the new woman leader. Think of this guiding coalition as your own personal cabinet. The ideal transition team provides valuable supplementary advice and resources just when you need them most.

The transition team is an advisory panel that helps you navigate the ins and outs of the new corporate environment until you are fully assimilated. Representing all areas of the organization, this team will serve as a vital communication link, sounding board, and feedback forum. Chosen and used well, it can be pivotal to maximizing success while minimizing risk.

JUMPSTARTER: *BUILDING YOUR TRANSITION TEAM*

Although many executives use a trusted group of their direct reports as a transition team, consider reaching beyond your inner circle. The panel should represent all staff levels and departments (including a labor representative if unions are a factor in your organization), giving you a more accurate assessment of how your leadership transition is really doing. Depending on your span of control, consider from 3 to 18 members.

If you were promoted, you will know the appropriate protocol for selecting a panel. If you are new to the company, learn how task forces and groups are typically created, and do your best to honor established practices to identify at least some of the participants.

Your transition team members should have the following characteristics:

- Respected by their colleagues (informal leaders)
- Confidant communicators
- Willing to be brutally honest in a diverse group of people
- Willing to serve as a communication link to their colleagues
- As a group, willing to provide a complete range of organizational viewpoints
- Committed to the success of the organization

Solicit ideas from your boss and direct reports about potential members. You may decide that you need all your direct reports involved and will add more members later. Reach out to the supervisors of potential members to gain their support for their staff's participation. Clarify time requirements (such as two hours every two weeks). If you are leading staff in multiple geographic locations, bring everyone together for at least the first meeting.

USING A TRANSITION TEAM TO JUMP-START YOUR WORK

Once assembled, your transition team needs a clear agenda and coherent goals. The team should help you learn the culture, test-drive your message, gain access to multiple perspectives, serve as a communication link, give you feedback, and help you identify early successes.

Learn the Culture

Organizations have histories that affect the ability of individuals to hear your message without distortion. Before launching a major communication effort, bounce your ideas off your transition team to see how the message will play. Do they think the audience (even an audience of one) will hear the message as you intend? The team can tell you what questions to anticipate and coach you on language or stories that tie into the organization's history and culture.

This is particularly useful when preparing for an important or difficult conversation. A transition team can help you avoid potential faux pas that a newcomer would never think of.

For example, a police chief launched his first week on the job by speaking to the command staff, often referring to "sworn" (officers with a badge) and "nonsworn" (civilians). A quick check

---

TRANSITION TEAMS AS LIGHTNING RODS

There are circumstances when a formal transition team may be counterproductive. In highly volatile environments, you may spark too much resistance and mistrust if you aren't extremely careful. In such situations, seek advice informally from individuals you intuitively trust. If you float the transition team idea and get too much opposition, you may decide not to develop a team. If necessary, save your political capital for other challenges; there are bound to be plenty.

with his transition team before the critical talk would have warned him that the department had spent enormous effort creating a collaborative spirit by deemphasizing the sworn/non-sworn dichotomy. In a single speech, he seriously undermined a vital ongoing initiative, and as one lieutenant described, set the department back five years.

Test-Drive Your Message

The transition team will help identify cultural nuances and organizational baggage that could undermine the effectiveness of your communication. (For the sake of a word, a career was lost.) For example, a new executive bemoaned her efforts to introduce the perfect logo to promote hopes and priorities for the department. The three-pronged message of honesty, competency, and respect lent itself well to a triangular icon. The response to her excited declaration? Silence. An announcement of "We're having left-over tuna casserole for lunch" would have inspired more enthusiasm. The executive discovered only later that a consultant, who was recently fired after wasting thousands of hours and a huge budget, used the same triangle icon to promote a disastrous strategy.

Gain Access to Multiple Perspectives

By providing the full range of organizational perspectives, the transition team can paint you a more complete picture. For instance, your predecessor racked up a few catastrophic failures, and you'd like to understand what went wrong before launching your own initiatives. Senior executives may insist that staff refused to budge, while staff will swear that top management failed to follow through on commitments or acknowledge progress. You need all sides of the story to be prepared for similar situations down the line.

Establish a Communication Link

When your span of control is too large or your schedule is too frenzied to appear personally, use them as an avenue of positive communication. They can help you "spread the good word" throughout the organization and update you on staff response.

Gain Constructive Feedback

When you make a presentation to staff, the representatives from the transition team will let you know how your talk was received and provide suggestions for your next round of connections. Once you have developed mutual trust, the team can also provide useful feedback on your leadership style and choices. Do you micromanage? Not manage enough? Are you missing important issues? They will tell you what is contributing to or limiting your success.

Identify Early Wins

The transition team provides valuable insight regarding which early efforts may produce the highest results. Members can also advise you about what quick successes—the easy victories discussed in Chapter 5—will have the most profound impact on your credibility.

PROPER CARE AND FEEDING OF YOUR TRANSITION TEAM

First, you need to make operating parameters clear both to the team and the organization. Under no circumstances should the transition team replace the current management structure. Your transition team really has no formal authority of its own; it's a temporary advisory panel. Reassure team members that you're

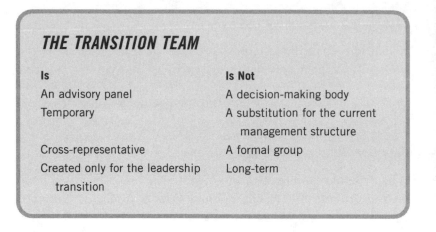

THE TRANSITION TEAM

Is	Is Not
An advisory panel	A decision-making body
Temporary	A substitution for the current management structure
Cross-representative	A formal group
Created only for the leadership transition	Long-term

accountable for your own decisions, and reassure those outside the team that this group doesn't represent a threat.

Transparency

Though individual outreach is sometimes necessary, discussions and decision making should be transparent. Avoid small gatherings or "committees." Keep members of your formal management team informed of the transition team's recommendations—perhaps by including them in the distribution list for minutes or other related documents.

Launching

In your first meeting with the transition team, clarify the team's function and set the tone. If trust is low in the organization, you should first ask questions that can be answered anonymously. Hopefully, you will quickly be able to move to open, productive discussion.

For example, using index cards or group discussion software, participants could answer the question, "How can we promote

WHAT'S IMPORTANT TO WOMEN

The transition team is a natural outgrowth of an inclusive management style that women typically prefer. First, women aren't as driven to establish hierarchy, rank, and power as men. They often prefer two-way communication and egalitarianism. Second, the "gamer generation" responds positively to a team environment. Third, new women leaders, particularly in a male-dominated culture, are more likely to face unproductive challenges to their authority. What better way to sidestep such a showdown than to include potential dissenters in your inner circle? The more closely leaders align direction and strategy with the desires of their staff, the more effective the ultimate implementation.

open, productive conversation in this group?" Display all of the anonymous answers, then have the group brainstorm around those answers.

The rest of the launch meeting should serve to outline the role of the team, identify tasks, explain your own hopes, and respond to group questions or concerns. Participants may come up with additional ways to be useful. Check Accelerator 6A in the Appendix for a sample agenda of a transition team launch meeting.

The most effective transition teams develop a strong rapport and group spirit. Encourage everyone—particularly field staff or frontline employees—to be brutally honest, especially when they disagree with the prevailing opinion. Everyone should check his or her rank at the door.

The level of rapport you gain and the overall comfort level of the group will directly affect the team's ultimate usefulness. The number of times you meet will be determined by your need

ELAINE'S TRANSITION TEAM

Elaine intends to draw on the accumulated experience of her transition team to better understand the political climate at the hospital. She will invite representatives from the nursing union, physicians' groups, department directors, and a board member to join so that she can thoroughly grasp a broad range of perspectives before making some tough financial and administrative decisions.

for information and the degree of change you expect the organization to experience with your transition.

WHAT IT ALL MEANS

Occasionally, transition teams will transform into semipermanent, ad hoc advisory panels after the transition period is over. If you decide to continue with the team in this way, consider rotating the membership. If all of your direct reports are members, you might also evolve the team into a more representative group, keeping your senior staff meetings separate. Remember to acknowledge the team's contribution to your leadership success once their tenure is complete.

Do not underestimate the importance of good advice in your first 100 days. Chosen and managed well, your transition team will help you build a rock-solid foundation for future success.

☑ *CHAPTER CHECKLIST*

- ☐ I have selected my transition team.
- ☐ Both the transition team and the organization know what to expect.
- ☐ The transition team feels comfortable giving me candid input and advice.

CHAPTER

The Second 50 Days

Until now, you've focused on gathering data, learning the work, developing relationships, researching quick successes, and managing your initial message. This chapter will provide you with several tools to organize your efforts, plan your next critical steps, and handle the challenges that emerge in the second 50 days. You've made it this far, but it's no time to coast. You still have a ways to go before securing a successful transition, and some of it will be uphill. But once you get up that hill, the view will be spectacular.

If you've followed your transition plan, you now have enough information to sink the *Titanic*. Your next steps are to refine the data, narrow your options, focus your efforts, and sell your plans to your stakeholders and constituents. You know what your boss or board expects. You know what obstacles you face. It's time to prioritize the work and craft your short- and long-term agendas.

Your first few months are the honeymoon stage. Time frames will vary, but one guarantee is that the bliss will eventually end. By now, you should have systems in place for taking care of yourself—and you should be prepared for the inevitable challenges.

Habits are tough to break, so develop good ones early. Regular exercise, ongoing meetings with a coach or mentor, or sacred times you keep for yourself are healthier patterns than missing meals or sleep. If your personal support system is not in place, now is the time to set it up. It's as essential as buckling your seat belt before the roller coaster starts. Establish good self-care habits now so you'll have them when times are tough and you need them the most.

Stay in touch with people who are important to your success. As you set your direction, keep them informed using agreed-upon communication paths. Describe issues or concerns and how you plan to resolve them. And don't forget to take credit when things go well.

In your second 50 days, you will need to do the following:

- Compare your original hypothesis to what you've learned on the job.
- Determine your priorities.
- Select your first win.
- Enlist support and build momentum for your plans.
- Continue building your team and other key relationships.
- Prepare for difficult conversations.
- Learn to deal with challenges to your authority.

JUMPSTARTER: *COMPARE YOUR ORIGINAL HYPOTHESIS TO WHAT YOU NOW KNOW*

Speaker and consultant Will Schutz used to tell his audience members, "There's the truth, and then there's the real truth." When you first start out, you may understand the problems and issues (the truth) but not the underlying causes (the real truth). By this time you should have a fairly comprehensive understanding of both.

For example, when Jeanne was interviewed to manage a large real-estate financing firm, she learned that one subsidiary was consistently underperforming and faced possible closure. The real truth was that the subsidiary had been consistently denied vital systems investment, attention, and information. The corporate cold shoulder was a major cause of the subsidiary's poor showing.

JUMPSTARTER: *DETERMINE YOUR PRIORITIES*

As you conclude your research phase, you should determine your priorities, decide on short-term wins or quick successes, and begin crafting your long-term direction. Referring back to the top priorities assigned by your boss or board, use the charts provided in Accelerator 7A in the Appendix to evaluate your next steps. Ideally, defining priorities separates the wheat from the chaff, refining data to help you identify the core ideas you need to rack up that first win and establish a consistent long-term direction.

As you develop your priorities, keep the following in mind:

• Your boss's or board's priorities. If your conclusions contradict those of your boss or board, polish up your persuasion skills, update your résumé, or prepare for a tough leadership challenge.

• The current strategic or business plan. Compare your research results to the goals and strategies of the company's plan, and resolve any discrepancies. Ask the following questions:

– What assumptions were used to create the plan? Are those assumptions still valid? What has changed?

– What current internal or external circumstances will affect the plan or its implementation?

If your organization lacks a clear business or strategic plan, develop one in your first year.

LIN CHOOSES HER FIRST WIN

As you recall from Chapter 4, Lin's primary tasks are (1) resolving the internal customer service issues, (2) tackling the politically charged technology issues, and (3) reducing the number of department grievances. She has direct control over the service issue, but the technology and grievance challenges will require cooperation and support from other senior staff. Lin realizes that a successful resolution of the service problems will net her the support required for overcoming the other challenges, so she chooses internal customer service as her first win.

- Organizational will. The credibility and leadership momentum you gain from your quick win will help you tackle the next major challenge. Therefore, save your toughest battles for your second wave of initiatives.

JUMPSTARTER: *ENLIST SUPPORT AND BUILD MOMENTUM*

Once you've established contact with key players, the groundwork is laid for gaining support for your plans. As you launch your agenda, respond to any concerns your boss has by explaining your strategy for overcoming obstacles. When deciding whose backing you need, consider those who must approve your decisions, those who are affected by your decisions, those who must implement your decisions, and those who can block your progress. Then get everyone on board. You should pursue support for your agenda with the tenacity of a politician hungry for votes. Shake hands, attend meetings, go to lunch, make calls,

ELAINE COMMUNICATES FOR SUPPORT

Elaine has chosen to outsource food services in the hospital as her first win. She uses the following table to determine her message.

Constituent	Their Priorities/Concerns	The Message
Boss/board	Hospital financial health	Food service will improve, costs will fall.
Nursing staff	Working conditions, patient care	Patients will receive better food on time; new service will improve working conditions once it's established.
Public	Patient care	Food service will be better; company will be accountable for quality.
Food service manager	Job security	Manager will oversee contract with food vendor, hospital will guarantee the manager's job for two years.

even kiss babies if you have to. Every ounce of effort now will pay off in pounds of organizational backing later on. Use the following ABCs for gaining support for your agenda.

- **Actively align.** Align your message with the needs and motivations of your key players. Determine whose support you require, and develop your message to speak to their concerns.

- **Build buy-in.** Convince your key players that you understand their issues and priorities. Show them how your agenda addresses those priorities. Let them know you understand their point of view and that you plan to act accordingly.
- **Communicate with confidence and conviction.** Your self-confidence and faith in your decisions will garner support. As one turnaround expert said, "People want to back a winner. You gotta look like a winner." Or in the words of a very successful consultant, "A strong opinion is worth 1,000 IQ points."

Tips for Getting Support for New Directions

Even if you have the best ideas since the microchip, you're going to have to promote them. It's the change, not the concept, that's tough to implement.

Broadcast Successes. Remind people of the good news. How often do you find yourself dwelling on problems that need fixing or areas that need improving? We often take our successes for granted and focus on the next dilemma to be resolved. Look for the good news in the organization, and publicize it.

Clarify and Emphasize What Is Not Changing. Tell stakeholders what will be maintained and protected from change.

Make It Easier. In some cases, you can propose a change as an experiment to make it easier for others to accept. If it is a difficult change, figure out what will make them resist it.

Show Empathy. Let your team know that you understand; let them know what's in it for them.

Tell Stories and Anecdotes. Concrete illustrations beam your message directly into the real world. Steve Sabol, son of NFL Films founder Ed Sabol, once recalled, "My dad always used to say, teach me and I'll learn, show me and I'll remember, but give me a story, and it will live in my heart forever."

For example, when promoting value-added service, Suzette uses an anecdote she learned while interviewing customers: "We didn't have the seat covers the customers wanted, so Laura in the auto shop gave them the names, addresses, and phone numbers for three other possible sources. We might have lost that sale, but the customers will remember Laura's integrity, and they'll be back."

Beware Statistics Overload. Well-placed numbers can grab employees' attention like a lasso, but too many numbers will make them feel like they're trapped in a vise or buried under an avalanche.

For example, reeling from "the peace dividend" in the late 1980s, a large naval shipyard was experiencing severe monetary problems. At a management meeting of more than 300 employees, the CFO made an extremely detailed presentation on the state of shipyard finances. After a grueling hour and 70 slides, the CFO finished his presentation, and the audience applauded loudly. Confused by the presentation and believing she had misunderstood critical information, a new employee leaned over to a colleague and said, "What did he just say?" Her colleague responded, "I don't know. He does this presentation at every meeting and we always clap." The CFO was promoting fiscal responsibility, but the message was lost after the third slide.

Use Symbolic Gestures and Short, Powerful Messages. As mentioned in Chapter 5, symbolic gestures and short, crisp messages are a powerful way to sell your agenda. They may be micro in size, but they can have macro-level impact.

ELAINE'S SYMBOLIC GESTURE

When Elaine entered the first negotiation with a disenfranchised union, she noticed that the oval table had management facing off against their union counterparts. She deliberately chose to sit on the union's side of the table. This was a powerful gesture to labor that the rules of engagement were changing.

JUMPSTARTER: *A CRASH COURSE IN TEAM BUILDING*

If you want to build a ship, don't herd people together to collect wood and don't assign them tasks and work, but rather teach them to long for the endless immensity of the sea.

—Antoine de Saint-Exupery

Over the past 25 years, I've worked with hundreds of groups, ranging from multimonth wilderness journey participants to the executives and boards of major companies. Even though each group had vastly different members, goals, and dynamics, they shared certain characteristics common to all team anatomy. As a result, I've learned three absolute truths about teams.

1. Teams That Start Strong Are More Likely to Ultimately Succeed

Teams move through a maturation process to arrive at optimal performance. Groups naturally travel through several stages, including a period of conflict. Your job as team leader is to help guide your team through these phases as efficiently as possible.

Whether it's the city symphony or a professional football team, the quality of the first few meetings can have a lasting impact on the group's long-term performance. A thoughtful agenda for Day One will help you start strong and maintain team energy.

The first 50 days are the "ritual sniffing" stage, as one friend of mine calls it. Many conversations during this period are shallow or noncommittal, but there is plenty going on at the unspoken level. Members are engaged, but they are privately wondering what the new team will be like, how much of their discretionary effort they want to invest, and how they fit in. They may feel some anxiety, and they are looking to you to give them direction.

The team meetings you held in the first 50 days should have helped to set the right tone and guide members into the next stage. These meetings should have included the communication of your anchors, the development of group norms, and the setting up of expectations for the team. In the second 50 days, it is possible your team dynamics will begin to shift. You can use your anchors as a way to shepherd the team through its "growing pains."

During this second stage of team development, hope bumps into reality. The excitement of having a new leader ebbs. The velvet rubs off to display some rough edges. You'll notice a subtle jockeying for power, frustration between individuals, annoyance at slow progress, or a questioning of the group's (and maybe your own) competence. Brace yourself. It's as inevitable as teething and just as uncomfortable.

Team-development theorist Bruce Tuckman called this phase "storming." Here are some typical examples:

- You feel a quiet tension in a meeting. Afterward, small groups cluster in animated conversation in the parking lot or around the latte machine.

- Sarcastic remarks or provocation replace open confrontation ("Hey, Sharon, to what do we owe the honor of your appearance?").
- Arguments erupt. When someone offers a new idea, others chew it up like hyenas setting on a wildebeest.

This phase is "group development hell." The team will be edgy, perhaps eager to blame. You are a likely target. You'll want time to make the right operational decisions, while they want leadership and action pronto.

To manage this phase, first keep in mind that it's perfectly natural. In fact, consider it progress. Remember, to get to that ideal level of high performance, the team must move through this phase.

People want to know what's next. If you can't tell them yet, let them know when you can. Suppose you are flying to Cleveland but get delayed in Chicago. Your annoyance grows in direct proportion to the lack of information the airline gives about the delay. Decide which message you would rather hear: "Good evening, ladies and gentleman. We have an unexpected delay. Please stand by," or "Good evening, ladies and gentleman. We have just heard from the cockpit that Flight 237 to Cleveland is delayed due to weather around O'Hare. We do not know the exact schedule but have set a departure time of 5:45 P.M. We will have an update for you in 15 minutes. We apologize for the delay."

Once you have successfully weathered the turbulent stage, the group will begin to relax. Differences of opinions will be discussed openly and respectfully. Team members will experience increased satisfaction, trust, and mutual consideration. If you reach this stage in your first 100 days, provide a lot of support and recognition for team members' accomplishments and keep them involved in decision making, including the creation of goals and standards.

WHAT'S IMPORTANT TO WOMEN

Women may take the storming stage personally—especially when the group is lashing out against leadership. Don't fall into this trap. Evaluate feedback within the context of what's going on with the team as a whole. If you are hearing the same theme consistently, if people you trust agree, and if the feedback resonates with you, then make adjustments. However, don't let the noise get in your way. You are guiding a group through a squall, and with persistence and a good sense of direction, you will get through to clear weather on the other side.

Remember from your assessment in Chapter 2 how you respond when cornered. Awareness of your negative reactions will help limit their effects. One executive I interviewed keeps a list in her right-hand drawer of behaviors she resorts to under extreme stress. She periodically refers to this list to make sure she's not instinctively acting out.

An aggravated group needs strong direction. This can be tough to manage if you haven't finalized your long-term agenda. Use these strategies to provide that "meanwhile" sense of direction:

- Reinforce your anchors.
- Remind the team of their agreed-upon norms, and recommit to them.
- Encourage the team to vent to release stress, but do not permit wallowing in negativity or "practicing misery." Discuss specific issues, then recommit to your direction.
- Develop short-term goals (like your first wins) or projects that stand a good chance of early success. If the first wins you select do not include the entire team, find other projects that you can work on with key players.
- Let team members know when you will have more information or a direction.

Of course, life and work are not linear. Changes in priorities, circumstances, or personnel can cause the team to bounce back to an earlier stage. However, with observation and responsiveness, you can accelerate their progress to higher performance.

2. Team Problems Don't Begin with Personality Conflicts

Team leaders often call and ask me to "fix" someone—a team member who just doesn't get along with colleagues. Most team problems are not about personality. They are usually the result of more fundamental, structural causes: lack of clarity or lack of alignment. If your team is experiencing tension or low performance, conduct the following diagnostic.

Clarity. Determine if each team member is clear on the following:

- Team goals and direction
- Individual roles—who does what, who is accountable for what
- How each team member contributes to the overall goal
- Systems—how the team gets the work done
- How members are rewarded for their accomplishments
- The decision-making process and the levels at which different decisions can be made
- How work flows through the organization
- Feedback—how individuals and the team are doing relative to goals
- The resources and information needed to do the job

Alignment. If these items are clear, then learn what is not aligned by asking yourself and/or the team the following:

- Do individual goals line up with team goals and strategic direction?

- Do the skill sets of individuals and the collective meet the requirements of the job?
- Does the goal reflect the team members' values?
- Do team members agree about the goal? About the approach? About the division of labor and responsibility?
- When there is disagreement, is it addressed with sensitivity and candor?
- Do existing systems support the team's work? For example, does compensation adequately reward people for the job required?
- Does resource allocation support the work that needs to be done?

If you can't answer yes to the questions, begin your team efforts by focusing on turning the "nays" into "ayes." If you can, then

WHAT'S IMPORTANT TO WOMEN

Women have an ability to effectively share power—an important factor in team development. We have a natural tendency to build community and entrust others. As Kira Porter writes in *Women Leaders: Strategic Yet Invisible Assets*, "Over the past 20 years, many organizations have become less hierarchical and command-oriented and are now flatter, more matrixed, more complex, and more team-dependent for high-quality results. Therefore the traits needed to lead effectively are also likely to be undergoing change. Evidence from a number of fronts suggests that women generally may come more easily to the critical leadership skills needed in this new, post-heroic model: communication, emotional intelligence, collaboration, negotiation, entrepreneurship, and coaching and mentoring."

perhaps it is appropriate to send your "problem child" to charm school.

3. Teams Without Common Goals Will Seek a Common Gripe

The most important way to accelerate a team's performance is to present a common, compelling goal. Conversely, if team members do not feel passionate about their objectives, or if protecting turf replaces collaborative efforts, they will find common enemies to rally against: labor versus management, nurses versus doctors, operations versus marketing, your staff versus you. One ideal example of unifying disparate groups to accomplish a common goal is the way squabbling agencies and departments must work together during an emergency or disaster.

JUMPSTARTER: *TACKLE TOUGH CONVERSATIONS*

If being in charge were always easy, you'd get bored. Eventually, you're going to face challenges that make you question why you took this job in the first place. Leadership sometimes leads to contention, and you need to be prepared for some tough conversations.

Kerry Patterson, Joseph Grenny, Ron McMillan, and Al Switzler, authors of *Crucial Conversations: Tools for Talking When the Stakes are High*, explain that difficult conversations have three components: (1) There is more than one opinion; (2) the stakes are high for at least one party; and finally (3) emotions run strong.

In other words, your stomach turns; your blood pressure surges, and you wish you could stuff envelopes for a living. By cosmic design, these conversations will occur when you are the most stressed and least prepared. Acknowledging tough conversations as a fact of professional life will help you get over—and even through—the worst of them with minimal amount of hassle.

Preparing for a Difficult Conversation

Most of us would rather get a colonoscopy than enter emotionally charged conversations. Here are some tips for managing the challenge of tough conversations.

Stall Until You Are Ready. If you can grab the time to prepare, do so. Often you can avoid being forced to talk when you're caught off guard. If it's a phone call, say you are in a meeting and set a time to talk later. If your boss storms in, be on your way to the restroom. Stall. Take a breath. Think.

Know Your Desired Outcome or Needs. By the end of the conversation, what do you hope will be different? What outcomes do you seek? These could be feelings, actions, attitudes, or beliefs. Perhaps you want the other party to understand why you are making certain choices. Maybe you want to lessen tension.

Remember to disagree agreeably. Maintain a respectful tone at all times. This helps keep the air clear of distractions, allowing everyone to focus on working toward a mutually satisfactory conclusion. All perspectives can be heard and considered. Tackling the issue without putting everything on the table is like trying to assemble a jigsaw puzzle without all the pieces. Use the form provided in Accelerator 7B in the Appendix to plan for your next tough conversation.

Delivering Bad News

Nobody enjoys delivering bad news, especially to someone who is liked and respected. Use the following guidelines to help navigate this dicey situation.

Prepare Yourself to Be Empathetic. Rick Brown, a successful consultant, is a master at delivering tough news while maintaining strong relationships. He recommends the following:

- Prepare yourself for the conversation by finding your own source of empathy. For example, let's say you must inform a staff member about his or her subpar performance on a specific contract. Think about those times that you failed to perform up to standards. This will help you minimize any tendency to sound judgmental.

- Come up with language that frames what you need to say, keeping the personality, values, and interests of the receiver in mind. What does he or she want? What are his or her fears? What reaction can you anticipate? Take these items into account as you plan how you will approach the conversation.

For example, Ronette, a new supervisor, was promoted over her best friend, Cheryl. Within the same year, Ronette was forced to tell Cheryl that she had been passed over for yet another promotion to senior level. Drawing on empathy for her friend and her knowledge of Cheryl's needs, Ronette broke the news this way: "Cheryl, this is probably tough for you to hear, but Delia was just promoted to senior. I know it's frustrating as hell and wish I could be giving you better news. When you're ready, I'd like to tell you what went into the selection criteria."

Choose the Setting with Your Audience in Mind. Consider the time and place from the recipient's point of view. Your office may seem comfortable to you, but it could feel like the warden's office to everyone else. If you're new, you may not be aware of institutional superstitions about "getting called to the boss's office." Choose a place where your message can be heard without your motives being suspect.

Choose Your First Words Carefully. If the recipient is not expecting bad news, you may have to preface your comments with a short explanation. Mark Fletcher-Brown of Reputation, Inc., writes in

600 Ways: A Collection of Ideas about the "Six Ways to Deliver Bad News." His advice is to begin with something along the lines of "I have some bad news for you about [x]. You may want to sit down. There are three things I want to talk to you about."

Be Brief and Direct. Do not say, "I'm thinking you could be doing a little better." Say, "Your performance is substandard for the following reasons. . . ." For example, on the eve of April 14, an accounting partner gave her exhausted assistant a 30-minute lecture about her performance. The assistant ceased paying attention five minutes into the monologue and quit the next day.

Let The Receiver Vent. It may be difficult, especially if his or her anger is directed at you. But remember, it wasn't you but what you had to say that caused the reaction. It's the news that blew the fuse, not you!

JUMPSTARTER: *DEAL WITH CHALLENGES TO YOUR AUTHORITY*

> Develop a second skin and treat it like a protective layer of clothing. If it's too thin, you'll get burned. Too thick (like a coat of armor), and you may not absorb important data about your leadership. When criticized, you need to feel a slight sting without suffering long-term damage.
>
> —Successful consultant

Eventually you're going to be challenged, either openly or covertly. It may be a schoolyard ritual to test your strength or an underhanded attempt to sabotage your position. How are you going to manage it? First, let's deconstruct the situation by looking at what makes challenges so, well, challenging.

Handle Open Confrontations

We don't fear failure. We fear exposure of our
vulnerabilities.

—Joan, labor union leader

An open or direct confrontation is often a deliberate attempt to
establish one-upmanship (or one-upwomanship). Women are
often turned off by hierarchy games and power plays, and they
are uncomfortable when forced to follow these competitive rules.

In addition, such challenges can touch off fears of inade-
quacy. Men and women both dread being exposed as incompetent and not having what it takes to lead others.

Women sometimes overreact. They receive standard criti-
cisms and suddenly feel that their career, relationship, or self-
esteem are also at risk. It is the equivalent of thinking that if
your husband won't mow the lawn, he doesn't love you.

The best way to manage these challenges is to keep them in
perspective. Keep the following strategies in mind if you start
overreacting or feeling defensive:

- Determine how your own lack of confidence affects the
  way you interpret the challenge. If you were someone
  else (such as Jack Welch, Mother Teresa, Attila the
  Hun, Roseanne Barr), how would you respond?
- Ask people you trust if your interpretation of the
  situation is accurate.
- Remember, you are in the lead. You can either play the
  game or change the rules.

If you decide to play the game, you must play to win. For
example, Mia was in a large meeting with her staff early in her
tenure when a disgruntled employee yelled out, "Do you earn
that big salary of yours?"

WHAT'S IMPORTANT TO WOMEN

Too often women seethe over harsh words or sarcastic comments long after the moment has passed. When in the military, my friend Chris was amazed to overhear two men arguing violently.

"You're an asshole!"

"No, you're the asshole, asshole!"

"Want to go get a beer?"

"Sure, let's go."

How would you respond if someone called you a bitch? My guess is you wouldn't buy him a beer. If you take criticism personally, you limit yourself. You have to learn from it and move on. Women don't become rigid and defensive—they become bitter, distrustful, or (worst of all) whiney, none of which are career-advancing traits. What a waste of talent.

Mia fired back, "I do, do you?"

She could have responded in a number of other ways too. She might have attempted to disarm with humor or self deprecation: "Big salary! Are you kidding me? I spend half of it on Maalox!"

Or by responding to the statement itself: "Sounds like you want to hear more about my job. How about the rest of you? Do you all want to learn more about my responsibilities and challenges?"

Or by addressing the real message head-on: "I can guess what's behind that question. I know you guys are frustrated at the changes being made. It's tough. But when we finally get through this tough time—and we will get through it—we are going to be fast and flexible. If we want to thrive in these current conditions, we'll need those qualities."

ALLIE HANDLES A SUBTLE CHALLENGE

After being promoted over the successful but complacent sales director, Dave, into a risky personal assignment with high corporate stakes and visibility, Allie knows many eyes are watching her. Dave begins "forgetting" to copy her on e-mails or to get other information to her on time. His social connections give him access to vital news, and he deliberately keeps her uninformed.

If Allie doesn't deal with this situation, she risks missing important data. If she overreacts, she may gain a reputation as a micromanager. It's a real tightrope.

First, Allie must deal with the omissions as quickly as possible. She should treat the first one or two slights as minor misunderstandings. Her hope is that she can win Dave over rather than come down hard on him. She might approach it like this:

Allie: Dave, I noticed that you didn't cc me on the regional update. If you'll recall, I asked you to copy me on all reports representing this department.

Dave: Sorry, my mistake. I'll do it next time.

Allie: OK, so we agree that you will cc me on external reports?

Dave: Sure, why not?

Problem apparently solved. But what if Dave pushes back on the cc idea?

Allie: Dave, I noticed that you didn't cc me on the regional update. If you'll recall, I asked you to copy me on all reports representing this department.

Dave: What's the big deal? I've been sending those reports for years. Bob [Allie's predecessor] didn't question them.

Allie: [still using an even tone] This isn't about questioning you. This is about me staying informed. I realize it is a change for you, and I appreciate the extra effort.

Dave: Fine, I'll try to remember.

Allie: So, you agree to cc me on your external reports?

Dave: That's what I just said.

Allie: Great. Thanks.

Now, what happens when Dave continues "forgetting" to copy Allie? Once a pattern develops, Allie should treat it as a performance issue. She wants Dave's commitment, but she may have to settle for his compliance. She articulates the performance gap using facts:

Allie: Dave, I have asked you several times to cc me on the reports. In the past week, you sent three reports without copying me.

Dave: This again?

Allie: [still using an even tone] I have made it clear that copies come to me. You have continued to miss doing this. What is going to help you remember?

Dave: I don't know.

Allie: Well, I need a plan from you regarding how you will keep me copied on the reports. Please let me know by closing time today how you intend to resolve this. Otherwise, we will need to set a regular meeting so you can update me on your activities.

Dave: I still don't know what the big deal is.

Allie: Dave, I have explained this. You and I don't seem to agree on this issue. I'm confident we can work through this. But for now I need your plan by end of day.

Dave: Yes, boss.

(continued)

> **Allie:** Good. I look forward to hearing what you develop. Now, how are things going on the Bradley account?
>
> In this case, Allie politely but firmly lets Dave know what the outcome will be if he doesn't come up with a solution to his performance problem. In these situations, a proactive maneuver is the best way to make sure that subtle undermining doesn't turn into a bad habit.
>
> Deal with a covert challenge only when it becomes a performance issue. Painful as it is, don't let the noise distract you. If you stay committed to your purpose, remain open to a healthy relationship, and reward those who come around to your views, you'll eventually garner the support you need.

Respond to Covert Challenges

Tougher to handle—and just as potentially damaging—are less direct, more covert challenges to your authority. Open rebellion is replaced by less volatile but just as lethal stealth tactics. An employee "forgets" to give you a vital piece of information. You hear about important breaking news from the wrong sources. Subordinates don't seem to work as hard on your shift and talk wistfully about your predecessor when you're within earshot. These small challenges are the "death by a thousand cuts" for your personal and organizational productivity (and sanity).

WHAT IT ALL MEANS

In your second 50 days, a mental shift will occur. It may come as a crystallizing moment when you suddenly and clearly envision the next year. Or it may gradually slip into focus. Whatever the process, the time for learning and planning eventually yields to positive activity and forward motion. To be effective, you'll need to finalize your immediate and long-term agendas, recruit support for your plans, and prepare yourself for the challenges that change brings. Know how to manage those tough conversations and subdue any challenges to your authority. and be sure to have your support system in place, because as the action truly begins, you are going to need every resource available.

☑ CHAPTER CHECKLIST

- ☐ I have compared my original hypothesis to what I've learned on the job.
- ☐ I know my first priorities.
- ☐ I have selected our team's first win.
- ☐ I have a plan for building support and forward momentum for our agenda.
- ☐ My support system is firmly in place.
- ☐ I know the steps I will take for building my team.
- ☐ I know with whom and how I will maintain strong relationships.
- ☐ I am prepared for whatever challenging conversations may be required of me.

The End of the Beginning

As YOU WIND down your first 100 days, you'll find that you've exerted enormous effort with little more than copious notes to show for it. This can seem frustrating and anticlimactic. Keep in mind that these early efforts will pay off—with serious interest—over the course of your leadership tenure.

The exact form the "end of the beginning" takes will be unique to your circumstances. Travel distances, attendance at special classes, and natural work cycles will affect your time lines. Your experience in the company, the industry, the orientation policy of your organization, and even vacation schedules will affect what you can accomplish.

JUMPSTARTER: *END YOUR FIRST 100 DAYS DELIBERATELY*

The first phase of your new leadership job will be over when all of the following have been accomplished:

- Your transition plan is complete.
- First wins have been determined and efforts begun.

- You know your agenda for the first year.
- Key personnel are identified. If you need additional expertise (such as legal, financial, or public relations), you have a plan for getting it.
- You feel a reduced need for your transition team.
- You have communicated the results of your first 100-day efforts to your boss.
- You have negotiated for additional resources you may need.

Of course, if leadership were as predictable as notes in a Day Runner, it would be far less interesting and challenging. If your first 100 days goes exactly as planned, congratulations. Guinness will be in touch about how to spell your name for the record books. But all too often, fate can gleefully disrupt your best-laid plans.

For example, Gloria began the chief of operations job at a medical air evacuation facility just a few days before a helicopter crash took the lives of a much-loved pilot and flight nurse. Her original 100-day plan was replaced with crisis response work.

The What-Ifs and the How-Dos

Whether your transition lasts three weeks or 300 days, this chapter brings the first phase (and this book) to a close. The important thing is to follow the activities described in earlier chapters as closely and efficiently as your circumstances permit. Before we sign off, however, there are some final, lingering questions to answer—what-ifs and how-dos.

What If My "Quick Win" Is a Loser? You may have placed your credibility on the line with your selection of first initiatives. Perhaps you underestimated resistance, or you severely overprojected how many sales your pricey promotion would generate.

OK, it's a setback. But you don't have to stay back. It's humiliating and painful, and you end up questioning why you took the job or ever thought you could do it. Your annoying inner critic amps up to say, "See, what did I tell you? You are incompetent!"

Get over it or get through it. There isn't a mistake you're going to make that some other very talented, smart, capable individual hasn't already made—usually more than once. There isn't a successful leader out there who hasn't made choices she later regretted. Experience helps; when you have seen things go horribly wrong before, you eventually learn that this too shall pass. You're going to survive, and you will be successful. I once heard an oil executive describe a conversation she had with a close colleague: "Yes, my friend, after all these years, we still have problems—but at least they are the same problems."

Exhibit leadership. Take responsibility but limit your self-incrimination. Treat the experience as a temporary detour, letting your integrity and purpose guide you. Identify what can be salvaged and what can be learned. You may have more climbing to do in order to prove yourself, but you can make it. Don't be afraid to admit you screwed up; just don't wring your hands while admitting it. Consider these hard-won pieces of advice from executives who've seen it all:

- Figure out what part of the effort was successful. What will you know next time? What have you learned, and how are you addressing the current situation? Include this in your communications.
- Take care of yourself. Treat yourself as you would your best friend. Make use of the support systems that you developed in Chapter 3. You did keep those up, didn't you?
- Tell it like it is, and tell it quickly, using short, clear statements. Don't let the drama distract you for long.

And don't get sucked in by others' inclination to "awfulize" the situation.

- Respond quickly but not rashly. Make sure you have enough information to make an honest assessment and create a rebound plan.
- Keep in mind that in the long run your loser could eventually be a winner.

For example, shortly after Bob was elected sheriff, his lieutenants pressed him to initiate disciplinary measures against a notorious employee. Bob's instincts told him that there wasn't enough documentation, but he took his staff's advice. He fired the troublemaker, who sued for wrongful dismissal and won—a painful slap to Bob in his first year. A year later, Bob now realizes that the respect and loyalty he gained from backing his lieutenants has been well worth the early setback.

Our corporate attention spans are getting shorter and shorter. Today's disaster will become tomorrow's stale news. Keep everything in perspective. You'll be off the radar soon.

How Do I Handle "Moments of Truth"? It would be nice if your challenges paced themselves with your learning curve, but you can't count on it. Eventually you will face moments of truth, when you must address a tough dilemma or conflict—and it may happen sooner rather than later.

Note Maryanne Peabody and Laurence Stybel's advice in their article, "When New Senior Executives Take Over":

Reserve the most important problems for the second cycle of change. We recommend first-cycle interventions focus on issues where there is a high probability of success. Your initial success then becomes a framework from which to build up for the next intervention. For example, in retrospect, President Clinton might have been better off FIRST getting the family leave bill signed into law and THEN tackling the issue of homosexuals in the armed forces.

If you can choreograph your moments of truth to follow directly after successful first wins, you will have a stronger management platform. However, if your early interventions are unexpectedly difficult, do what you must to win and prepare to compromise later.

How Do I Handle Changing Priorities? If your priorities change, so do your requirements. There are probably additional resources or time lines for which you should negotiate. You may need to limit the scope of other projects or put an initiative or two on the back burner. Change is inevitable, and priorities shift constantly. Be very clear with your boss or board about the ramifications of a shift relative to your other priorities.

Change is even more disruptive for your staff. If you are in a business or industry where there is constant flux, consider taking these proactive and responsive steps.

Proactive

- When setting expectations for your staff, explain that change will be part of the job.
- Let your staff know how you will personally respond to shifting priorities. Describe the steps you will take to keep everyone informed.
- Be aware of how your own emotional reactions to change.

Responsive

- Acknowledge what staff must be experiencing.
- Help staff reprioritize their work.
- Try to minimize other changes—now is not the time to move to a new location.
- If possible, deliver the news personally. Multiple messengers create multiple messages.
- Be ready for tough questions. Resistance is an uncomfortable but natural and healthy response.

- Use your transition team as a communication link with the rest of the organization.

As Elaine Bernard, professor at the Harvard Trade Union Program, explains, "Leading change is like driving a vehicle moving in deep snow tracks. You all know the organization should turn right, but to pull out of those tracks is tough indeed."

How Do I Know When I Am "In"? The first rule is to always behave as if you're already in. Remember, perceptions have a way of becoming reality. However, you'll know for sure you are in when you establish personal connections and when casual conversations include you. Are you part of the banter? Perhaps staff joke about blocking the door to keep you from entering. You are copied in the joke-of-the-day e-mail. People look for a way to have fun with you. You're in. Just be certain that the relationship building doesn't replace maintaining lines of authority when the need arises.

For example, Karen, a human resources manager, feels like the rule maker for good behavior. She is involved in antiharassment efforts in the public sector and must confront other senior managers about their oppressive behaviors. When they began affectionately calling her "Sister Mary Karen," she knew she'd been accepted.

In essence, you're in when people accept you and engage with you. The conversation or energy level doesn't shift down when you join the group. Colleagues seek you out to vent or ask your opinion. Others want to involve you in their conversations and activities. People listen to your ideas and give them a proper vetting.

Warning! Don't fake an interest or try to artificially become "one of the guys" just to fit in. Find real ways to connect. If everyone else hunts and you're an animal rights activist, don't try to talk turkey calls. Your colleagues and staff can sense that kind of inauthenticity a mile away, and you'll say good-bye to your credibility. Find other activities and interests that you can really share.

And what if you never feel accepted? Don't get worked up about it. Getting in is just a way to make your job easier. It's a means to an end, not an end in itself. As Diane, a successful biochemist, said when describing her experiences breaking into a male-dominated medical school, "I knew many of the male faculty didn't want me there. I just never let it take up a lot of my attention." In other words, find something more productive or interesting to focus on.

What If I Am the First Woman in the Job or on the Team? If you are the first female to "make it," congratulations. Now is the time to take advantage of being different. You have something unique to bring to the table, and it's not just your manicure.

For example, Amy was a project manager of a large transportation firm and the highest-ranking woman. She took advantage of being different by joining female networking groups and associations. In bidders' conferences, men did not consider her a threat and often gave her proprietary information that put her group on the cutting edge.

If you take a hit, don't obsess. Channel your frustration into something productive or let it go; in other words, use it or lose it. Women who hold on to their anger over a particular injustice often get stuck. Get up and get back in the game. Don't take it personally. Your tenacity will pay off.

SEVEN HABITS OF HIGHLY EFFECTIVE FEMALE LEADERS

I have interviewed many amazing women as part of my research. In my conversations with company presidents, CEOs, mayors, fire chiefs, and admirals about their first 100 days, I learned as much about "how to be" a female leader as I did "what to do." There are certain intangible qualities that may be hard to categorize, but they're worth pursuing and incorporating into your own leadership journey. So, you ask, what do the women leaders who were interviewed have in common?

1. **They are able to balance their concern for others with self-advocacy.** They can negotiate on their own behalf and on behalf of their team, but they still maintain a strong sense that the ultimate decision has to feel fair.

2. **They are excellent technicians.** They often move up the ranks by excelling at a highly technical endeavor (pilots, engineers, and so on). As one military officer said, "Flight checkouts are neutral. How could they question my ability when I tested first in the class?"

3. **They are powerful communicators.** They know how to get their message across the first time, and they avoid the communication errors discussed in Chapter 5.

4. **They always feel left behind.** One executive agreed with the words of her colleague: "When I die, I will still be behind." They have learned that their lives are chaos and that they will never have complete control. They make peace with doing the best they can.

5. **They don't feel limited by their gender.** Most of the top executives I interviewed don't consider being female an obstacle. However, many of them cited examples of the limitations it placed on other women and how those women limit themselves. They didn't allow comments such as "We don't think women belong here" to faze them. Similar to Diane, the biochemist quoted earlier, they don't let detractors take up a lot of their time or energy. In fact, they are often able to turn strong naysayers into coaches and advocates.

6. **They swallow their fears and grab the risky, highly visible assignments.** They feel self-doubt but don't obsess over it.

Incidentally, research shows that women are more risk-averse than men, but they perform just as well in risky conditions. And if given a lousy assignment, interviewees made the best of it. As one admiral mentioned, "I often received window-dressing assignments because I was a high-ranking woman. I just made the best of them while actively seeking new assignments too."

7. **They keep their sense of humor.** Whether leading in a crisis or interacting with a demeaning jerk, top female executives find the lighter side of otherwise dark and stressful circumstances. They can laugh at themselves and manage to keep things in perspective.

HOW TO KNOW YOU'RE ON THE PATH TO SUCCESS

It's still early to tell whether your agenda will be successful in the long run. However, if you've followed the directions provided in this book, your chances are very good. Here are some positive signals to watch for:

- Your words are being echoed, which means your message is coming through.
- When you check, the line staff is clear on your priorities and direction.
- Regular meetings with your boss are productive and positive. He or she supports your long-term direction.
- You like your job and look forward to next year.

If you are getting these good vibrations, then I have one last piece of advice for you.

JUMPSTARTER: *CELEBRATE!*

Give yourself a break, kick up your feet, and pop the cork. Take the rest of the night off. But it's back to work tomorrow. As Carrie Fisher said, "There is no point at which you can say, 'Well, I'm successful now. I might as well take a nap.'"

Your first 100 days have come to a close. Your transition plan is complete. You have launched your first wins and begun selling your long-term agenda. You know your key people and have a plan for maintaining your relationships. After a successful start, you feel a reduced need for your transition team and your boss knows what a great job you've done. You've kept your sense of humor and managed some tough transitions. Good work, and congratulations on a successful first 100 days!

☑ CHAPTER CHECKLIST

- ☐ My transition plan is complete.
- ☐ First-win efforts have begun.
- ☐ I know our agenda for the first year.
- ☐ I know the additional expertise I need and have a plan for getting it.
- ☐ I feel a reduced need for my transition team.
- ☐ My board or boss knows the results of my first 100-day efforts.

EPILOGUE

Why Organizations Should Care About the First 100 Days

A FIRST LOOK at demographic trends may cause decision makers to shudder. In the next few years, there will be a radical departure of management talent across all industries, so expect major leadership shifts. For example, *The Nonprofit Quarterly* stated in 2002 that between 10 and 12 percent of the 1.6 million nonprofit organizations are managing an executive leadership transition at any given time. That number is expected to climb, with 61 to 78 percent of leaders expected to leave within five years. Virtually all of my clients, in both the public and private sectors, are facing an unprecedented exodus at the leadership and management levels.

Alert leaders can take advantage of the coming shortage. Management transitions are pivotal moments in an organization's life; paying attention to them makes excellent business sense. Leadership vacuums may cause instability, but they also present the smart executive with white-space opportunities for positive change. Such volatile times have potential for accelerated success or major setbacks.

Careful planning and management of transitions is an important strategy. However, despite ample evidence supporting the creation of an integration plan, less than 30 percent of newly hired executives receive one. Because so many organizations do an abysmal job of managing transitions, those that can get it right have a decisive competitive edge.

The likelihood (and cost) of transition failure is high. As the Center for Creative Leadership (CCL) notes, 30 to 50 percent of high-achieving managers (those who have reached at least the general management level) are fired, demoted, or reach a career plateau. In the CCL's words, "Estimates of unwanted turnover due to derailment costs run from six figures at middle management to seven figures at the senior executive level."[1] Compare that to the cost of support and development. Why would any sane organization *not* do more than give a new leader an office, a password, and a good-luck wish? You might as well wind up a toy car and point it toward the closest brick wall.

A thoughtful transition plan will help maximize success. And with all the leadership positions that will need to be filled in the next five years, businesses are going to need to have such plans in place. The following key steps should be included:

• **Prepare the organization before the transition.** Make sure the environment is ready for the new arrival. This is particularly important if you are planning a concurrent change initiative. Openly declare your plans for change to the organization at large well before the new leader begins. When the inevitable resistance emerges, be sure to support your new leader despite any personal discomfort this may cause in the short term.

• **If the transition precedes a major change initiative, announce that initiative ahead of time.** Don't set the new leader up as the lightning rod for unpopular but necessary programs.

---

1 Michael Lombardo and Robert Eichinger, "Preventing Derailment: What to Do Before It's Too Late," Center for Creative Leadership, 1989; reprint. 2001.

- **Evaluate how the new leader will fit the role relating to business strategy.** If there are critical skill gaps, be prepared to help fill them.
- **Tell it like it is, especially when "the emperor has no clothes."** Don't let your efforts to sell the job prevent you from providing critical success information to candidates.
- **Engage the new leader immediately.** Discuss results of the interview process, suggest opportunities for making connections with critical stakeholders, and establish a routine for frequent initial check-ins.
- **Stay involved and supportive until the new leader has cemented her position.** Avoid jumping to conclusions. Don't disengage until she agrees that she has solid relationships throughout the organization. Be the high-level backup.

WOMEN LEADERS MAKE GOOD BUSINESS SENSE

Deloitte-Touche research proved that by promoting training and development for executive women, the company saved $250 million. It makes good business sense to create an organizational culture in which women thrive. Yet too many organizations are not taking advantage of this opportunity. Failing to help women maximize their potential is like keeping cash in a mattress—a terrible waste of a perfectly good resource

Women are underutilized. Even though 46 percent of the workforce is female, only a pathetic 10 to 15 percent of women make it to senior staff positions, and only 3 to 5 percent are top earners. Women are leaving Fortune 500 companies at twice the pace of men, but they remain determined to contribute to organizational life. And they do. Despite the challenge, or perhaps because of it, women have made remarkable strides. There's a place in both the kitchen and the cabinet, and for good reason.

Research shows that the traditionally inclusive female style has also been "shown to produce better worker performance and effectiveness in today's world."[2] Progress is being made slowly, and the next generation is more accustomed to seeing women in charge. The more we do to accelerate the advancement of women, the more profitable our bottom lines will be.

It's smart business, but what's it really going to take for females to advance properly? A close friend and former manufacturing executive quips, "A lot of dead white men." I am more hopeful, and I believe that organizations can play a critical role in helping worthy women succeed.

The best training is unofficial. Formal programs, career planning, and courses provide good *schooling*, but the best *education* comes from easy rapport and unofficial coaching. Women still lack ready access to the breezy shoptalk that men enjoy. There are exceptions, of course, but the overwhelming majority of women do not benefit from the casual networks that develop at ball games, on the golf course, or around the watercooler.

An egalitarian promotion policy alone is not the answer. When delegated authority appears gratuitous, women will face resentment and questionable credibility. Ultimately, responsibility without legitimate authority causes burnout. If corporations are going to maximize their investment, they should pay close attention to the effective, comprehensive development of *all* employees. Women in senior positions, like their male counterparts, are role models for everyone in the organization.

One acquaintance was offered a teaching position at a military academy. She held the rank of captain and had more than 20 years of service, but she had to ask the question, "Is this assignment gender-related?" The assignment officer said, "As a matter of fact, it is. We need female role models for our female cadets." The captain quickly responded, "No, actually it's the *male* cadets that need female role models."

---

2 "Women Most Effective Leaders for Today's World," EurekAlert!, American Association for the Advancement of Science, August 4, 2003. Press release.

How to Encourage and Support Women Leaders

- Assign sponsors to fast-track women. These advocates must be influential and truly believe in their mentee's potential.
- Create opportunities for informal but genuine connections.
- Encourage women to actively develop informal networks and mentors.
- Present the business case for comprehensive, organizationwide development, then create a tailored approach for implementation.
- Weave together the ideas of value and diversity when crafting the organizational fabric.
- Sponsor nongender-specific activities. Replace the annual golf game with a barbeque.
- Promote an environment that facilitates work-life balance.
- Recognize the additional pressure put on women who have families; often, catering to their needs (such as providing on-site day care) benefits both female and male employees.
- Encourage executives to take a brutally honest look at their organizations. Are the administrative and clerical positions held predominantly by women? Are the higher-paying operational positions held predominantly by men? Such practices limit the company's ability to hire smart women at the executive level.

Once recruited or promoted to a leadership position, women can benefit from high-level support and informal coaching even more than men. Women also flourish when they have someone they can vent to about professional and emotional challenges. Ongoing feedback from multiple sources (especially in a strongly male culture) helps reinforce a woman's assessment of her own impact and effectiveness. Finally, it's critical that women leaders have equal chances to steer highly visible, high-profile projects to successful completion.

Women have repeatedly demonstrated the *ability* to lead. Today's organizations must create the settings in which talented women really *want* to lead. By recognizing and encouraging potential stars, effectively supporting leadership transitions, and maintaining systems that promote workforce diversity, decision makers will guarantee both a robust leadership pipeline and continued long-term financial success.

100-DAY ACCELERATOR 1A: QUESTIONS FOR CONDUCTING DUE DILIGENCE

You will have learned plenty about the organization and the job while interviewing for your position. Use the following questions to see what learning gaps you still need to fill.

Questions to Ask Your New Boss

☐ How did you select me for this position?
☐ What is your management philosophy?
☐ Whom can I talk with to give me a sense of your management style?
☐ What three things do you currently do to support your direct reports?
☐ What types of problems do you want to be involved in resolving?
☐ When was the last time someone challenged the status quo? What happened?
☐ How are people developed within the organization?
☐ Who are my peers, and what do they do?
☐ What are the characteristics of a successful person at this company (or in this position)?
☐ Who are the key players with whom I should connect?

Questions to Ask Your New Peers

☐ If you were talking to your best friend, how would you describe what it is like to work here?
☐ How do people communicate here?

- ☐ How would you describe the level of teamwork? How important is teamwork?
- ☐ How well do people get along?
- ☐ What is everyday life like in this organization?
- ☐ What are the biggest challenges you currently face? Opportunities?

To Learn About Performance

- ☐ What are key performance indicators/goals, and how well is the company/department/team doing relative to those indicators?
- ☐ What is the company's current financial situation?
- ☐ What are the company's driving factors for success (mission, people, product, strategy)?
- ☐ Describe some emerging opportunities and challenges.
- ☐ How is good performance determined, and how do people know when they have achieved it?

Operational Issues

- ☐ Explain the current organizational structure—how it's supposed to look on paper and how things really are.
- ☐ How are the most important decisions in the company made?
- ☐ How effective are current operations?
- ☐ How are current resources allocated and managed?
- ☐ What supports good performance here? What obstructs it?
- ☐ How does the organization respond to change?
- ☐ How would you describe the organization's ability to learn and evolve?

The People and Culture

- ☐ How would you describe the predominant leadership style in this organization?

- [ ] What worked or didn't work about my predecessor's style?
- [ ] What role do you think my predecessor should play in my transition?
- [ ] Who are my key contacts? What is the best way to develop a relationship with them? What is their relationship to one another?
- [ ] How would you describe the political climate within the organization?
- [ ] What will it take to develop employees' trust in a new leader?
- [ ] What is the precedent for female leadership?
- [ ] How has the past influenced the current situation? What have been significant moments in the organization's history?

100-DAY ACCELERATOR 1B: FIRST IMPRESSIONS

Measures of Success	Initial Impressions
I have a clear understanding of the following: • How success is measured • How the department/organization is doing relative to objective measurements • How knowledgeable parties perceive current operations History: • I have an initial concept of how the organization's history could impact future efforts.	

(Continued)

- I understand the driving factors that have contributed to what the organization is today.
- I know significant events the organization has recently experienced.

Operations	Initial Impressions

Current Operations:

- I have a theory about current operational strengths and weaknesses.

Future Operations:

- I know opportunities and threats that could impact our future.

Personnel and Culture	Initial Impressions

People:

- I have an initial impression of what it will take to develop credibility and trust from key players.
- I know the relationships among key players.

My Boss:

- I have a good idea of what it will be like to work for my boss.

My Predecessor:	
• I know the appropriate relationship to have with my predecessor. • I know what my predecessor's role should be in the transition.	

Stakeholders	**Initial Impressions**
The Board: • I have a good initial understanding of the goals, roles, processes, and expectations of the board members, including how decisions are made. • I understand the board dynamics and political nuances.	

100-DAY ACCELERATOR 2A: TAKE A GOOD LOOK AT YOURSELF

Use the following questions to determine your capacity and strategies for taking charge in your new leadership position.

Past and Present

- As you think about your career, what makes you feel particularly proud? When have you felt the most alive and in sync with your own purpose?
- What skills and traits have contributed to your success? What are your unique strengths?
  - Professional—general skill sets (such as financial, technical, operational) and leadership skills (such as

setting an example, inspiring others, big-picture focus, building the capacity of others)
- Personal (such as tenacity, charisma, creativity, flexibility, competitive spirit)
- What strengths might you tend to overuse in this new job? What strengths might you underuse?
- When have you been the most uncomfortable in your career?
- What attracts you to this new job? What scares you about it?

Future

- What are your professional and personal hopes and dreams for the position?

Working Conditions

- Under what conditions do you feel the most confident and powerful?
- What circumstances contribute to your highest level of productivity?
- When do you have the most fun?
- Think of the times when you bring your best, most creative self to your work—when you are both happy and productive. What circumstances contribute to that? What does that tell you about what you value and enjoy doing?
- What kind of team brings out the best in you?
- What else contributes to your best potential work experience?
  - Physical layout of your workspace
  - Priorities—of both the organization and your colleagues/management
  - Work atmosphere

Understanding Shadows, Automatic Responses, and Intuition

- What are the physical indicators that let you know something isn't right (for example, stomach pains, racing pulse)?
- What happens when you get scared? How do you respond? How do you interact with others?
- How do you react when under extreme stress?
- How do you respond when your authority or credibility is questioned? How do you handle open challenges, confrontations, and criticism?
- When your back is against the wall, what are your automatic responses? What triggers alert you to these responses? What can you do to minimize the negative consequences of such behavior?
- What counterproductive things might you do when scared or stressed?
- What can you do to manage your negative reactions? What support do you need?
- Is there a pattern to things you tend to avoid? Why do you think that pattern exists?

Working with Others

- In its 2003 "Women of the Year" issue, *Ms.* magazine celebrated high-achieving women who "raised our spirits, renewed our faith, elevated our discourse, and rocked the boat." What impact do *you* need to have in your new position?
- How do others bring out the best in you?
- What is important to you about how people interact with one another?
- What role do you typically play in conversations or meetings? How does it contribute to or distract from a productive result?

- How you tend to manage conflict?
- Ask a trusted colleague who knows you well to describe the following and compare your perceptions with hers or his:
  - Your leadership style
  - The impact you have on others
  - What you do to bring out the best in others
  - The role you typically play in conversations and meetings and how it contributes to or distracts from productive results
  - The extent to which your actions contribute to or distract from a productive result from others
  - How you tend to handle conflict

Authenticity

- Imagine yourself in a work environment where your image is comfortable and you feel free of all pretenses. What factors contribute to that level of comfort?

100-DAY ACCELERATOR 3A: MY ENTRY PLAN

Entry Plan

- I know what success looks like and how my performance will be evaluated during both my first 100 days and my first year.
- I have a workable communication plan with my boss or board.
- I understand what my boss and board consider the strategic issues to be.
- There is an entry plan in place so that I can learn both the key business issues and players.
- I have received input about the most important things I need to learn.

Agreements

I have the following agreements in place:

- How and when I can exchange feedback with the appropriate people
- Clear roles, responsibilities, and boundaries for myself and my subordinates
- An effective support system, like a mentor or executive coach
- The ability to renegotiate for resources once I have learned more

Observations

- Based on my observation of meetings, I have a theory about the way things get done around here.

100-DAY ACCELERATOR 3B: UNDERSTANDING YOUR ANCHORS

Consider your answers from Accelerator 2A: Take a Good Look at Yourself, then answer the following:

- What values or principles are important to you in the workplace?
- What codes of conduct are necessary for you to thrive in any leadership position?
- What is important to you about the way people treat one another?
- What is important to you about the way people approach their work?
- What do the preceding answers tell you about your anchors, your working absolutes?

100-DAY ACCELERATOR 3C: MY SUPPORT SYSTEMS

Support to Consider	What I Need	How to Make It Happen
Social/emotional		
Spiritual		
Physical		
Professional		

100-DAY ACCELERATOR 3D: PREEMPLOYMENT NEGOTIATIONS TOOL

Desired Situation	+ = Must Have o = Should have n = Nice to have	Reasoning
Staffing		
Budget		

Resources		
Board/boss expectations		
Other		

100-DAY ACCELERATOR 4A: EXAMPLES OF TEAM NORMS

The following are examples of team norms that groups have chosen in their first meetings.

Our team agrees to do the following:

- Vet all ideas respectfully, regardless of the source.
- Balance our need to be heard with the need to listen.
- Disagree respectfully.
- Deal with issues before they become problems.
- Before making a major decision, we will ask ourselves these questions:
  - Does the decision align with our vision?
  - Is the decision fair?
  - Will the decision make us a better organization?

When we meet, we will follow these guidelines:

- One speaker at a time; we discourage side conversations.

- Everyone participates equally.
- Everyone is responsible for the effectiveness of the meeting and the quality of the discussion.
- Interruptions should be for clarification only.
- Express interests without attacking or blaming others.
- Listen to understand, suspend judgment, and give each idea a fair hearing.
- Accept conflict and its resolution as necessary for progress.
- Follow through with commitments between meetings.

Examples of additional agreements:

- We return e-mails to one another within a business day.
- Staff meetings are the number-one priority.
- If someone must miss a meeting, he or she will notify us ahead of time and be responsible for getting briefed on the decisions made.

100-DAY ACCELERATOR 4B: SAMPLE FIRST TEAM MEETING AGENDA

1. Introductions, if necessary

2. Acknowledgement of change; appreciation for what is going well

3. Your background, if necessary
   a. Personal
      Family
      Interests
      Schooling
   b. Professional
      Career path
      Successes
      Setbacks

4. Your hopes
   a. What you would like stakeholders to be saying a year from now

  b. What success means for you a year from now (what is expected of you)
     Working climate
     Operations
  c. Your hopes and assumptions for the team

5. Request for team response
   a. Their own personal and professional backgrounds
   b. Their interests and passions, what excites them
   c. Their concerns and what about the job keeps them up at night
   d. What brings out the best in them and what they want from leadership

6. Your leadership agenda
   a. The kind of workplace you want to promote
   b. Your personal vision
   c. How staff should interact with you and each other
   d. Your moral "absolutes," your anchors
   e. Anything else they should know about working with you
   f. What you want to know about working with them (Follow up in one-on-one meetings.)

7. Mini–strategy meeting
   a. Report of what you already know (your working hypothesis)
   b. Their initial response
   c. How your time will be spent and your availability
   d. Plans for a transition team (Get response.)
   e. Description of your entry plan
   f. Your performance expectations, broadly speaking

8. Reinforcement of your excitement, optimism, and commitment

100-DAY ACCELERATOR 5A: LEVERAGE YOUR RELATIONSHIPS

Leveraging your leadership will require establishing trust and credibility as quickly as possible. Use the following chart to consider what you need to learn from key players and what they need from you.

Who	Learn Early	What You Should Do	What They Want to Know
Bosses	• Strategic direction • Top five tasks or outcomes (yours and theirs) • Boundaries of responsibilities • Who they think your key relationships are • Their communication preferences • Their hot buttons and quirks • Limits of your decision-making authority • A possible "early win" • What they consider a success • The best way to get resources (How difficult is it?)	• Avoid surprises. • Negotiate personal access.	• How you plan to keep them informed • That you have what it takes • That you will deliver on your commitments

Senior team members	• How performance is currently measured	• Quickly assess individual performance and capabilities.	• What's expected of them
	• How decisions are made	• Acknowledge the change, challenge, and the work done to date.	• Whether they still have a job
	• Individual strengths and weaknesses	• Make sure your decisions are performance-based.	• Whether they can trust/respect and rely on you
	• Company history	• Be candid and clear about goals.	• The limits of their decision-making authority
	• How they see their roles and your role	• Avoid interrogations.	
	• Their hot buttons and quirks	• Avoid quick personnel decisions and consider all	
	• Key relationships (feeling supported or not-supported, etc.)	the options (e.g., fire, move, demote, special projects).	
	• Common journals or books they read	• Establish relationships.	
	• Their take on the business climate (strengths, weaknesses, opportunities, threats)	• Let them know you need them to be successful.	
	• The accuracy of your hypothesis about each department		
	• A possible "early win"		

(Continued)

Who	Learn Early	What You Should Do	What They Want to Know
Staff members	• How well they understand the mission and how their work is linked to it • Informal systems and relationships • A possible "early win" • What has worked/not worked with past initiatives • Changes they would like to see • Roadblocks to getting work done	• Get out to see them early in your tenure. • Find out if perceptions in the ranks are shared and consistent with those of the executive team. • Let them know you need them to be successful.	• Whether their contributions will be acknowledged • What's changing and what's remaining the same • Whether you have their interests in mind • Whether you will let them do their jobs in the best way they know • Whether they can believe in you • Whether you accurately understand their dilemmas
Transition team members (see Chapter 6)	• Access to the "real" story • Organizational norms • Response they need from you when giving bad news	• Clarify that this is a temporary assignment. • Ask for brutal honesty and unsolicited advice.	• Expectations of their role and time commitments

	• How open the establishment is to discussing tough subjects. Which topics are "undiscussables"?	• Get recommendations about who should be a member. • Clarify with others the purpose of the team.	• Decision-making clarity (i.e., whether they are only making recommendations) • Whether their names and comments will be kept confidential • What will happen with the information they give you
Board members	• Expectations • Existence of multiple political agendas • History • Their hot buttons and quirks • A possible "early win" • Relationship to the institution	• Clarify board roles and boundaries. • Negotiate access to members.	• How you plan to keep them informed • That you will offer no surprises
Customers	• Their perceptions of the level of service • What happens when the system works	• Meet personally with your most important customers (internal and external) early in your tenure.	• Your plans • Your interest in solving their issues

(Continued)

Who	Learn Early	What You Should Do	What They Want to Know
Customers *(continued)*	• What needs to be improved • A possible "early win" • What's important to them about how they do business with your product or service		
Shareholders	• A possible "early win"	• Ensure the transition is clearly communicated.	• That you have what it takes
Unions	• Their influence in the organization • How their power is used • Bargaining history (e.g., interest-based, traditional) • What is working/not working • History of labor/ management relationships • What they want • A possible "early win"	• Learn the history of labor relations for the company. • Meet with local leaders as soon as possible. • Include union reps early in budget discussions that affect bargaining units • Seek assistance from union on matters directly affecting operations. (Workers are in the best position to help, if asked.)	• Your background in labor/ management relationships • The level of honesty or disclosure to expect • If you can be trusted • If you will rein in wayward supervisors • If you treat workers with dignity and respect

100-DAY ACCELERATOR 5B: MANAGE YOUR MESSAGE

Situation You Expect to Enter	Confirming Behaviors	Outcome Needed from Your Message	Specific Actions to Take	Other Ideas
Climate				
• Crisis of confidence	• Employees seem stuck and are unable to be proactive.	• Recommitment to organizational goals	• Be visible. • Be clear about direction. • Show your strength. • Communicate bad news quickly, then focus on the future. • Communicate early and often. • Create short-term plans.	• Conduct a "reassurance road show" by visiting the job sites and personally talking to staff • Conduct daily stand-up meetings or huddles.
• Low level of trust	• Staff won't talk in meetings; there is little conversation, an overall sullen demeanor, and a sense of disenfranchisement.	• Trust in leadership	• Get people from different factions in the same room. • Conduct large meetings or cross-department conferences early on.	• Invite all the appropriate stakeholders to the table. • Create a website that allows anonymous posting of employee

(Continued)

Situation You Expect to Enter	Confirming Behaviors	Outcome Needed from Your Message	Specific Actions to Take	Other Ideas
		Climate		
• Low level of trust *(continued)*			• Bring disparate groups to the table. • Open up meetings; allow employees to ask questions anonymously. • Add employee questions to standard meetings. • Build teams. • Encourage conversation. • Link personal and organizational efforts to the vision.	questions, and be quick to respond openly and honestly. • Connect your message to staff interests. • Use and formalize the rumor mill. • Doughnuts in the hallway • Be sure employees realize that what they think matters; focus on their contributions. • Emphasize honest communication. • Be transparent about authority.

• Discouragement, low morale	• Employees are focused on the way they are treated.	• Hope	• Focus on the future with easy wins. • Encourage everyone's involvement. • Rebuild morale by cleaning up the workplace or acquiring important resources. • Plan activities early on that encourage pride.
• Chaos brought on by fast growth or rapid change	• Staff are burned out, confused, and change-weary.	• Focus	• Set priorities quickly. • Ensure clarity of top management and corporate goals. • Reinforce the vision. • Limit changes as much as possible. • Articulate what is not changing. • Acknowledge staff efforts. • Minimize and simplify your message to one goal.

(Continued)

Situation You Expect to Enter	Confirming Behaviors	Outcome Needed from Your Message	Specific Actions to Take	Other Ideas
		Climate		
• Chaos brought on by rapid decline or downsizing	• Employees are experiencing denial, fear, unrest, and a loss of productivity.	• Hope	• Conduct planning meetings. • Make quick, visible strikes of progress.	• Make your first cuts deep enough that further cuts can be avoided.
• Healthy setting	• Everything is OK.	• Maintain performance	• Celebrate and recognize staff and company achievements. • Explain what's next.	• Do not make unnecessary changes. • Create a theme for building on success.
• Complacency	• Staff have a "not my job" attitude, are committed to processes that don't work, avoid responsibility, and make it	• Reenergize	• Set aggressive goals. • Evaluate incentives.	• Emphasize urgency. • Focus on problems to be solved.

	difficult to conduct serious conversations.		
• Replacing a popular leader	• Staff compare your style to that of past leadership.	• Commitment and loyalty to the organization	• Have the outgoing executive introduce you and discuss why you were selected. • Emphasize what won't be changing. • Don't personalize the comments that compare you to past leadership.

100-DAY ACCELERATOR 5C: COMMUNICATION PLAN WORKSHEET

Use the following chart to build your message by articulating who you are, constructing your message, and identifying your audience.

Who You Are

What are the anchors you will convey
in your first communications?

What do you know about your
communication style and patterns?

What do you need to keep in mind
as you craft your message?

Your Message

Objectives: What do you want to
accomplish (e.g., promote action,
a feeling, awareness,
commitment)?

1.

2.

3.

What message do you need to
convey?

Methods/Channels: What are the most effective methods and channels for delivering your messages to different audiences (e.g., written, oral, e-mail, paper, in person)?

1.

2.

3.

How is the organization set up for communication? Are those avenues appropriate for your message?

Symbols: Are there other, more creative ways to deliver the message? If so, what are they?

Your Audience(s)

Who needs to receive the message?

1.

2.

3.

What does your audience care about?

How can you tie your message to what is important to your audience?

100-DAY ACCELERATOR 5D: POTENTIAL FIRST SUCCESSES

Use this chart to identify and evaluate some possible "early wins."

Potential First Success	Likelihood of Success Within 100-Day Time Line	Visibility (internal and external)	Level of Support from Key Players (including transition team)	Investment Required

100-DAY ACCELERATOR 6A: SAMPLE AGENDA FOR TRANSITION TEAM LAUNCH MEETING

1. Thanks to volunteers for participating and to their supervisors for allowing them sufficient time

2. Purpose of the transition team
   - To maximize the success of the transition while minimizing the disruptive effect on staff by serving as
     - A communication link to the rest of the organization
     - An advisory panel to new leadership
   - To provide a range of organizational opinions and viewpoints

3. Team's role and decision making
   - Team as a complement (not a replacement) for the current management structure
   - Your serious consideration of their input as you make strategic and operational decisions

4. Team structure
   - Meeting schedule
   - Time lines
   - Other administrative details (including their level of access to you)

5. Team questions (If trust is low, answer questions anonymously.)
   - What agreements must we make so that we can have open, productive conversations? (Often these agreements involve issues of confidentiality.)
   - What must I, as a leader, do to allow the team the freedom to be brutally honest and give me candid advice that contributes to everyone's success?

- What short-term success could mobilize and inspire this organization?

6. Entry plan
   - If appropriate, ask the team to review your entry plan (Remember that your schedule will be very full; if they recommend additional activities, they should also propose what to table or eliminate.)

7. Review of next steps and closing

100-DAY ACCELERATOR 7A: PLANNING THE NEXT STEPS

Task/Expectations	Current Reality/ Challenges	Next Steps
1.		
2.		
3.		
4.		
5.		

Use the charts that follow to organize your thinking about different aspects of the organization.

	Analysis	Next Steps
Objective measures of success		
Degree of customer satisfaction		
Predominant leadership style		
Level of board/boss involvement		
Political climate		
Resources		

(Continued)

	Analysis	**Next Steps**
Budget		
Team productivity/ motivation		
Individual productivity/ motivation		
Organizational/departmental strengths and weaknesses		
Labor-management relationship		
Organizational culture		

Department	Strengths	Weaknesses	Emerging Issues and Other Considerations	What's Needed (maintain, recalibrate, invest)	Your Expectations

Rising Issues and Other

Personnel	Strengths	Weaknesses	Considerations	Options	Your Expectations

100-DAY ACCELERATOR 7B: PLANNING FOR DIFFICULT CONVERSATIONS

What do you hope will be different at the end of the conversation? What outcomes do you seek?

Feelings

Actions

Attitudes or Beliefs

AN INVITATION: LET'S KEEP LEARNING

If you have comments, questions, stories, ideas, or feedback, or if you would just like to discuss this book, please contact us at info@100days.com.

Liz Cornish has been a professional speaker and trainer for more than 20 years. Contact her at liz@100days.com for a current list of keynotes and training topics. Keep checking our website for products and other 100-day resources.

INDEX